*This book is dedicated to Bill Byrne, friend
and mountaineer. You are sadly missed.
1953-1999.*

MUNSTER'S MOUNTAINS

30 Walking, Scrambling and Climbing Routes

Denis Lynch

The Collins Press

Published in 2001 by
The Collins Press
West Link Park
Doughcloyne
Wilton
Cork

© Text Denis Lynch 2001
© Maps David Lynch 2001

British Library Cataloguing in Publication data.

Typesetting by The Collins Press

Printed in Ireland by Colour Books Ltd.

ISBN: 1-898256-17-9

Front cover image: Looking down at Lough Akinkeen from the top of the
northeast gully, under Knockboy.
Back cover image: Pitch-climbing on Howling Ridge as seen from its neigh-
bour, Pipet's Ridge.

CONTENTS

INTRODUCTION

Ireland, unlike north Wales or the Highlands of Scotland, is not renowned for its mountaineering routes. Our topography and geographical make up is different and it is seldom we get hard winter conditions to allow us to climb on snow and ice. However, we do have mountain routes, and they are unique in their own right. There is enough varied ground to train Irish climbers for the world stage, or at least provide a sound background for it. What we have we must make the best of, and this guide has been written with two objectives in mind:

1.) Going up mountains on routes which involve more than walking but nothing too severely technical. The experienced hillwalker who has aspirations to move on to a slightly more technical terrain on the Irish mountains will find this useful.

2.) In a spirit of exploration, bringing one on to a different aspect of the mountain environment and providing an alternative perspective which can be very rewarding.

Grading: The term 'scrambling' will crop up a lot and in its simplest description means hands have to be used on difficult or steep ground. A scramble should not exceed rockclimbing grade 'moderate' and even at this level rope protection should be used. In my opinion if the level of difficulty reaches rockclimbing 'Diff' then the route has moved into the lower grades of rockclimbing and the proper level of experience, competence and equipment is required. Scrambling will be described adjectivally using the terms *Easy, Moderate,* or *Hard* and these should not be confused with rockclimbing classifications.

British adjectival grading will be used to describe any

rockclimbing in this guide and they will take in four grades, *Diff,*
V. Diff, Severe and *Hard Severe*. In my opinion, a climber would
want to be climbing at least one grade and preferably two grades
above the grade of rockclimbing on a mountain route as opposed
to climbing on a crag, because extra clothing, big boots and ruck-
sack will increase the difficulty on the stated grades, not to men-
tion changing weather conditions, loose rock, grass sections, poor
protection, etc.

If a route is described using the Scottish system then it will go
from Scot Grade I to II taking in two levels. A Scot I is a simple
snow gully or ridge with no complications on it except possibly
for a corniced exit or a small ice step whereas a Scot II will be a little more difficult with a few small pitches of steeper ground or an
exposed ridge. Nothing in this guide will go above this level of
difficulty. If a route is described using this type of classification
then it can be taken for granted that it is a winter route. Given the
uncertainty of the terrain on most of the routes in the guide, grading can be mutable at best so allow for this before doing a route
and always err on the side of caution.

Maps: The Ordnance Survey maps, 1:50,000 scale, should be used
at all times and for some areas such as The Reeks, a 1:25,000 scale
is available and this gives very good detail. Any sketch maps used
in this guide are only for the purpose of identifying areas and cannot be used on their own. They are not drawn to scale.

Equipment: A route may have special equipment needs and this
will be stated in each description. For general scrambling I always
take 20 metres of 8mm walking rope, some slings and karabiners
for safety reasons even if they do not get used, just in case an
'easy' scramble turns into something more formidable.

Access: Access has been well established by now to the more popular places but all due care should be taken not to damage walls,

fences, or disturb livestock (especially during lambing season) and not to trespass on private land. Traditionally, landowners have granted access to walkers but it is important to maintain their goodwill and to comply with any reasonable requests they might make. Never block gates or openings.

Timing: Times stated are approximate and will vary from person to person and according to the conditions of the day. I have been on all routes described and have endeavoured to give clear and concise information. However, all information provided must be combined with personal experience and good judgment. As the climbs take up only a portion of the day and can sometimes be done without taking in the entire mountain walk, routes may be shortened. They can also be lengthened or combined where appropriate and again this is up to the user of the guide. Personally, the walk and climb come as a package.

Route Description: The summary of each Route will provide salient information at a glance. The Grid Reference given is where to park the car and before a single step is taken. This summary information is then followed by a description which will cover general route finding, dangers, areas to avoid, some alternatives, etc. Compass bearings must be used when navigating on the mountains as it is not enough to follow a general description such as 'head southwest'. The guide is not saturated with information detailing every metre of a route but rather as an aid to one's own mountain skills. The heading *Terrain* refers to any technical or semi-technical sections, whether snow and ice climbing, rock-climbing or scrambling. These can change because of constant erosion on the mountains or when people of diverse abilities choose to tackle a section in a way different to that described in the book. Some routes will have a *Caveat*, which has been put in to point out a portion of the route which is particularly dangerous and most likely cannot be protected. I have tried to be objective about descriptions but my own preferences and biases will crop up from time to time. Any feedback is welcome.

Photographs: I have used photographs to give the guide a strong visual content. Their primary function is to provide information for the user to help identify terrain and routes and are taken, for the most part, relative to the particular approach in question. The guide, therefore, is designed to be used on the actual day's outing as well as choosing and studying the routes beforehand. Some photographs are taken to give overall views of the landscape which can be useful also. If some of the photographs go beyond the requirement of information provision and become vaguely aesthetic then this also serves a purpose as it begins to demonstrate the visual impact this kind of environment has on the viewer and how overwhelmingly beautiful the mountains are.

A Final Word: There are many reasons why people venture into the hills, be it for walking, climbing, fell-running, photography, etc, but the common denominators should be for the love of them and the sheer enjoyment of being there. Please observe the golden rule and leave the countryside as you find it. Enjoy the experience.

Disclaimer: Mountaineering can be a hazardous business and no responsibility can be taken by the author or publisher of this book, should any mishap or accident occur while on any of the routes described.

ACKNOWLEDGEMENTS

To name all the people who contributed to the creation of this book would make an extensive list. Suffice to say they know who they are, as they know how grateful I am for their participation, generosity, expertise and most of all their tolerance.

Míle buíochas do gach aon duine.

LIST OF MAPS

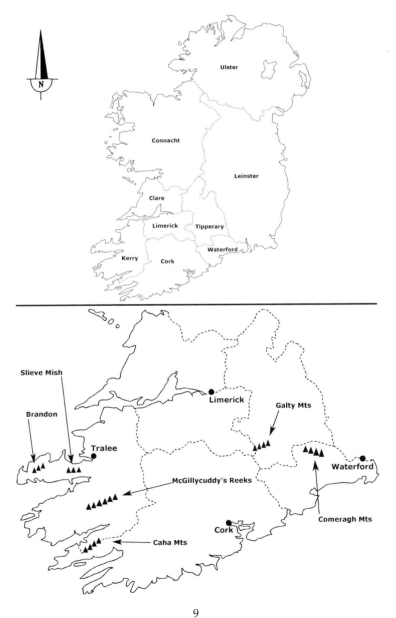

SYMBOL DESCRIPTIONS

■　　　= Start

▲　　　= Height

⬭　　　= Lake

═══　= Road

───　= River

▬▬▬　= Ridge Line

· · · · · · · ·　= Route

ROUTE 1
THE CIRCUIT OF COUMSHINGAUN – SOUTH-WEST GULLY – WINTER

Distance: 7km   *Ascent:*600m
Time: 4.5 hrs   *Terrain:* Scot grade II
Ref.: O.S. Map 75   *Start:* S341102
Equipment: 9mm or 11mm rope, ice axe, ice hammer slings, karabiners and crampons needed.

On the main Dungarvan/Carrick-on-Suir road, the R676, there is a parking spot and picnic area clearly marked, 16km from Carrick-on-Suir and 10km from Lemybrien. This is the starting point for both Coumshingaun and Coum Iarthar. It is the most obvious gully in the south-west corner of the coum and it exits onto the plateau.

Leave the car park, go through the wood and pick up a forest road. Turn right and follow this road as far as a fence. Cross the fence and turn left following a path with the fence and forest on the left. When the fence turns left, veer right, away from the fence and move towards the shoulder of the southern ridge. The path can become vague at times so keep in mind that the direction is northwestwards to the lower slope of the ridge and be careful not to go too high onto the ridge. Contour west into the coum keeping to the southern side of the lake which is at 385m above sea level. Walk right to the back of the coum and ascend to the starting point of the gully. NOTE: I have called this route 'the south-west gully', but this describes its position in relation to Coumshingaun. It is actually facing northeast. If the area has not frozen then this section will have to be bypassed by going to the left and moving higher up the face. Crampons, rope, axe and hammer are needed and slings are adequate for protecting the initial difficult move. The hardest part of the climb is at the start and it becomes straightforward after that. The turf will freeze as well as the water and provides perfect conditions for using the ice axe and hammer

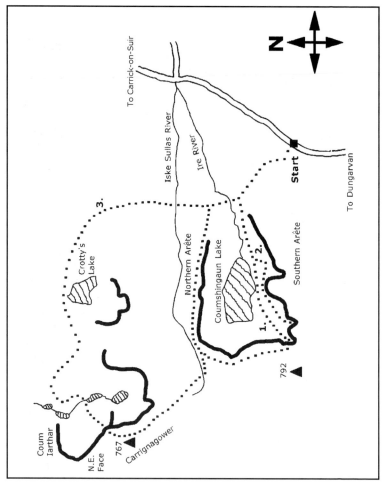

on steep ground. There are three options to exit and the middle one is the easiest. To complete the circuit of Coumshingaun follow the coum north for less than a kilometre and then turn east to go down the northern arête. From here there are good views of the north-facing wall and the options on it. Descend the ridge and head south to pick up the original route on the southern shoulder and back to the start.

At the south-west end of Coumshingaun, starting just above the lake, and trending diagonally to the right.

ROUTE 2
THE CIRCUIT OF COUMSHINGAUN AND THE TWO NORTH GULLIES

Distance: 7km   *Ascent:* 600m
Time: 4.5 hrs   *Terrain: Easy* to *Moderate* scrambling. Two
                                        moves of *V. Diff* rockclimbing
Ref.: O.S. Map 75   *Start*: S341102
Equipment: 8mm or 9mm rope, slings and karabiners needed.

Walk into Coumshingaun using the same approach as for Route 1.
    Stay on the east side of the lake and approximately 500m from
the south-west gully and 65m above the lake is the entrance to the
first gully. The start is a *V. Diff* rockclimbing move in a wet and
vegetated corner. The slab is good for gaining initial height before
making the next move up. There is a good spike to belay the second and after this there is a *Moderate* scramble move before the
ground becomes just a steep walk. Halfway up the gully, exit to
the right and traverse under a face of vertical rock and walk to the
entrance to the second gully after 400m. There is another *V. Diff*
move at the entrance and though it is always wet, the move can
be protected with two sling placements. Continue with some *Easy*
and *Moderate* scrambling in a very vegetated gully. The exit is just
below the final 50m of the southern arête. There are some *Easy*
and *Moderate* scramble moves on the arête and it can be exposed.
Otherwise move to the left and follow the path onto the plateau.
Continue as for Route 1 to complete the circuit of Coumshingaun.

Route 2

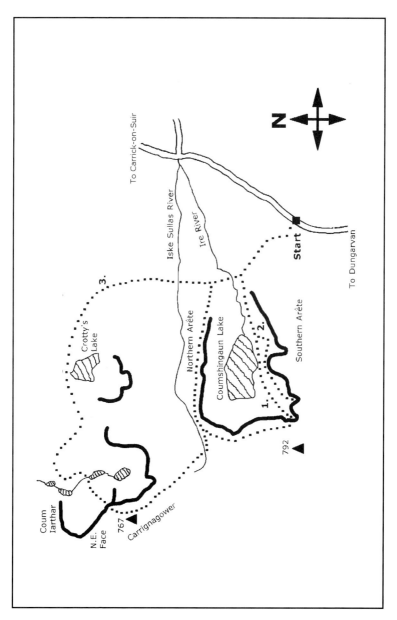

Two north-facing gullies with a traverse right under an impressive crag.

ROUTE 3
COUM IARTHAR – THE LONG NORTH-EAST GULLY

Distance: 9km | *Ascent:* 600m
Time: 5.5 hrs | *Terrain: Easy* to *Hard* scrambling, some moves of *Severe* rockclimbing
Ref.: O.S. Map 75 | *Start:* S341102

Equipment: 9mm or 11mm rope, full range of rockclimbing equipment, climbing harness, helmet, slings and karabiners needed.

Start as for the previous two routes but instead of going into Coumshingaun, cross the Ire and Iske Sullas rivers and contour around the broad ridge between Iske Sullas River and Crotty's Rock. It is worth going this route to Coum Iarthar just to see the imposing rock formation above Crotty's Lake. Staying at an elevation of about 300m, continue around to the entrance of Coum Iarthar, cross a fence and follow it until it veers to the right. Cross it again and ascend southwest towards the north-east face, passing near the second highest lake. The face runs for 500m between an arête at the start of the upper lake and a broad ridge which curves down to the third lake. The face has impressive gullies and rock pinnacles and the gully in question here is well-defined and runs the full height of the north-east face. The start is the most difficult and should not be attempted in wet conditions.

A good belay position can be set up by ascending steep ground a little to the left of the gully which will enable the lead climber to swing into the gully below the belay position. This move, though awkward, is rewarded by a solid quartz vein.

This quickly runs out and it is necessary to climb dubious grass on the left with no protection. A short distance up there is a good belay stance under a vertical wall of about 4m. This first, short pitch is the most difficult in the gully and is graded at *Severe* rockclimbing, but a *Caveat* has to be issued that it cannot be protected. Using the left corner, climb the next short pitch, graded at *Severe* rockclimbing, which can be adequately protected. After this

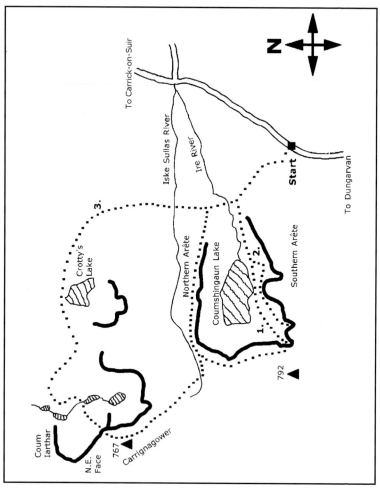

pitch, climb roped up together as the ground can become steep with several *Hard* scramble moves. The final portion of the gully involves just two awkward sections of *Hard* scrambling. The first is a slab between 4m and 5m high, which is stepped and poses no great difficulty though is always wet and is followed by a short steep section of grass which leads to the next *Hard* scramble move. This angles to the right, under a slightly overhanging wall.

*A difficult start to the north-east gully
which exits onto the plateau.*

Walk on steep, broken rock to the top which is a short distance
away. Cross the plateau to the northern arête and descend as for
the previous two routes.

ROUTE 4
KNOCKAUNAPEEBRA – MAHON FALLS

Distance: 7km   *Ascent:* 500m
Time: 5 hrs   *Terrain:* Scot grade II and *Easy* to *Moderate*
                                   scrambling
Ref.: O.S. Map 75   *Start:* S314081
Equipment: Crampons, ice axe, ice hammer, 9mm or 11mm rope, ice
screws, harness, extenders, slings, karabiners and helmet needed.

On the main Dungarvan/Carrick-on-Suir road, the R676, there is
a turn off at Mahon Bridge for Mahon Falls. Park the car at the car
park, which is at 380m. Walk along the track to the falls which is
1km away.

OPTION 1: It is seldom the entire falls freeze up and on the occa-
sion this route was followed only the bottom section was frozen.
Halfway up the falls move to the left to a gully which is about
15m high and a little harder than it looks, though not harder than
Scot II. Climb out of this and move higher to get above the falls
before traversing over to the south-west face, contouring for
about 200m until the entrance of the gully is reached. It is marked
by an impressive needle of rock on the left. At this point the elevation is 490m. The gully is *Easy* scrambling with two moves of
Moderate on good slabs, the first being halfway up and the second
near the top. The gully is approximately 100m high and makes a
nice approach to the twin cairns of Knockaunapeebra at 726m.

To complete the circuit head west to get to the spot height of
744m which is less than 2km away. Change direction, following
the rim of Coumfea to get to the next height marked 717m. Turn
southeast and walk across the bog to the cairn at 668m. At this
point there are impressive views of Coumtay and the south-west
face of Mahon Falls. Continue down this ridge heading southeast
and directly back to the car park. Though the overall distance is
7km and the ascent just 500m, I have given this outing 5 hrs to

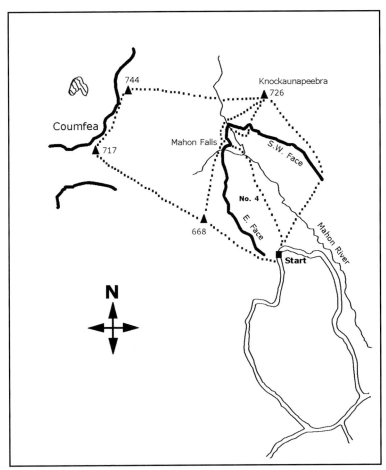

provide for pitch climbing on the falls which can be slow. The falls do not come into condition every year and in a situation like this it is a case of 'seize the day'.

OPTION 2: This is the same route except that it is a summer option and so conditions will differ considerably.

Start as already described and scramble on the left side of the falls. The scrambling is mixed from *Easy* to *Hard* but be careful not

A scramble up on the left side of Mahon Falls and traverse to the gully on the south-west face.

to misjudge this area as it is simple to end up on something more difficult than scrambling. The gully exit mentioned in Option 1 is too wet and slimy to do in non-freezing conditions so move to the left of it and scramble on grass and rock which is *Easy* scrambling, until the exit move which is *Hard* and a little awkward, though not high. Continue to ascend above the falls and then traverse over to the south-west face. Complete the climb by ascending the gully and if the plateau is wet then it is better not to do the circuit already described. One option is to descend the ridge from Knockaunapeebra heading southeast and then turning southwest after 2km on the ridge. Cross the Mahon river and back to the car park. The second option is to cross over to the western side of the falls and descend this ridge, also heading southeast and directly back to the car park. By going down this ridge there are good views of the south-west face and the gully just climbed. The information given in the summary is for the full circuit.

8mm or 9mm rope, slings and karabiners are needed for the summer option.

ROUTE 5
GALTYMORE BY LOUGH DIHEEN – NORTH-FACING GULLY

Distance: 11km   *Ascent:* 800m
Time: 4.5 hrs.   *Terrain: Easy* to *Hard* scrambling
Ref.: O.S. Map 74   *Start:* R875279
Equipment: 8mm or 9mm rope, slings and karabiners needed.

One of Ireland's Munros, Galtymore, is situated in the Galtee Mountains, which straddle two counties, Limerick and Tipperary. This 25km-long range goes from Anglesborough in the southwest to Cahir in the northeast and is a very popular destination for hill-walkers. The fertile Glen of Aherlow runs parallel on the north and the Knockmealdown mountains are 15km to the southeast.

There are only two routes chosen from this range that suit the brief of this guide book but in the proper winter conditions many more routes may become accessible to the aspirant mountaineer. Nevertheless, it is an area well worth visiting.

Turn off the N8 just outside Mitchelstown on the Cahir side and drive on the R513 for 6km. Turn right for Anglesborough and after a further 5.5km beyond Anglesborough, turn right at the Barna Cross Roads and drive for 6km to Clydagh Bridge. Turn right and ascend this road for a couple of hundred metres and park the car in an obvious parking area on the left. This is a popular parking spot especially for hillwalkers doing the Cush/Galtymore horseshoe. Walk along the road for 2.5km and go through a gate onto open ground. Head south-southwest for Lough Diheen, the coum between Galtybeg and Galtymore. There is a well defined, north-facing gully to the left of the cliffs, which goes up to the col between the two peaks. The gully is 150m high and is mainly *Easy* scrambling with the occasional *Moderate* move and one *Hard* but short section a little more than halfway up. At this point the gully is bisected by a large, wedge-shaped rock and the *Hard* scramble move is on the mossy slab to its left. Near the

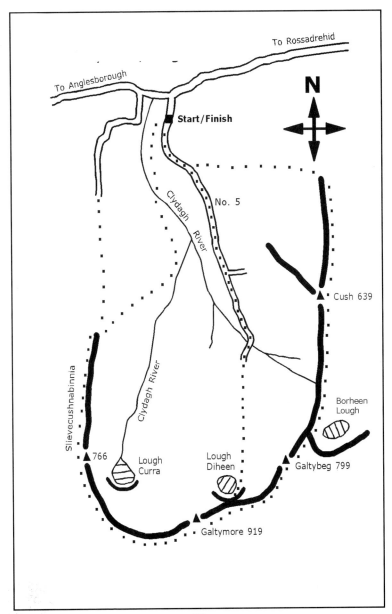

The distinct north-facing gully over Lough Diheen exiting between Galtybeg to the left and Galtymore to the right.

top of the gully there is a series of rock buttresses. Move to the right and continue up this fork, taking care as there is some loose rock before reaching the col. From the col head southwest for the top of Galtymore and continue in the same direction for 700m approximately, descending to 820m before changing direction to the northwest and gradually descending to Slievecushnabinnia at 766m. From here move down the north-northeast ridge to a track which meets a road west of the Clydagh River. Descend to the main road, turn right and walk back to Clydagh Bridge. Alternatively, come off the ridge about 1km from the top of Slievecushnabinnia and head northeast to a forest track which will meet up directly with the parking area.

An alternative to going by Galtymore and Slievecushnabinnia is to go by Galtybeg and Cush. At the col, head northeast for Galtybeg and from the top descend north-northeast to the col and ascend north to the top to Cush. Continue north as far as the forest and change direction northwest and descend to the road. Walk down the road a little to the parking area. If taking this route then the *distance* will change to 9.5km, the *ascent* to 830m and the *time* to 4 hrs.

ROUTE 6

GALTYBEG BY LOUGH MUSKRY – NORTH-EAST GULLIES

Distance: 13km   *Ascent:* 790m
Time: 5 hrs   *Terrain: Easy* to *Hard* scrambling
Ref.: O.S. Map 74   *Start:* R923282
Equipment: 8 mm or 9 mm rope, slings and karabiners needed.

Drive past Clydagh Bridge as far as Rossadrehid village and turn right at the post office. Drive up this road for 1km before turning sharply right. Park 300m from the sharp turn, opposite a forest road. Walk up this road and turn left onto a larger forest road. Follow this past the Galtee Waterworks into the Muskry Glen. After walking for 3.5km to Lough Muskry continue along the east side of the lake to the upper lake.

OPTION 1: Three gullies present themselves and the distinctive north-east-facing gully is on the right and divides the north-east facing cliffs from the north-west-facing cliffs. It provides a route up to the rock formation called O'Loughlin's Castle, 200m above. The gully is straightforward with some *Easy* scramble moves, usually in wet conditions. There are no route-finding difficulties as it is a case of just following the stream and ignoring a brief deviation in the gully to the right, three-quarters of the way up.

OPTION 2: The second option is to climb the central gully. Walk up the ridge which divides the central gully and the left-hand gully until it is necessary to contour a little into the gully to the right. There is an obvious, wet step shortly after entering the gully and it is necessary to bypass this by climbing a *Moderate* scramble move to the right. Enter the gully again and walk up to a short, *Hard* scramble move over wet boulders. Walk on steep ground to a division in the gully. The right fork is just a steep walk, while the left fork provides some difficulties. If taking this, there are some

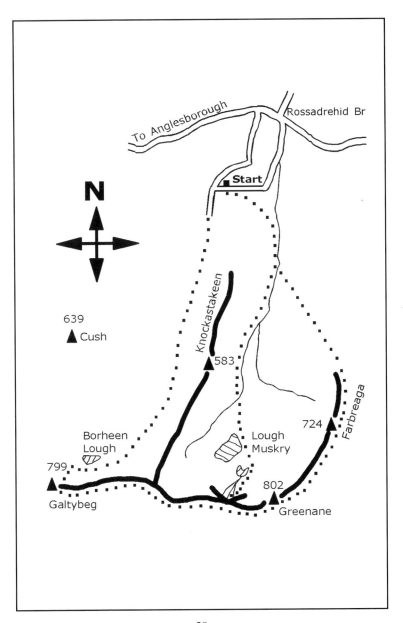

The three north-east-facing gullies all converging at a common boulder-field just above Lough Muskry.

Easy to *Moderate* scramble moves before a *Hard* move on broken ground below the top section of the gully. Avoid the upper section and make a short, *Hard* scramble move to the right, to get onto the ridge. Make a *Hard* scramble move over some rocks on the ridge, but this can be bypassed by going to the right and some *Easy* scrambling to get above this.

OPTION 3: This is my favourite option, though only marginally more difficult than the central option. Approach as for the central gully and traverse to the left. Avoid a wet step initially by climbing to the right on steep ground and in a shallow gully running parallel to the main gully. It is mainly grass with some mixed scrambling. Avoid another wet step in the main gully by continuing on the right until above it and then move back into the main gully. The gully narrows, with impressive rock walls on both sides, but it is just *Easy* to *Moderate* scrambling to the top.

From O'Loughlin's Castle move west-northwest to the height mark 786m and continue in generally the same direction to the col between it and Galtybeg. Change direction slightly and ascend west for the peak of Galtybeg. Descend north-northeast to the 500m contour line just above the col between Galtybeg and Cush. Contour around by the Lough Borheen coum to avoid the forest plantation and then head in a northeasterly direction to meet the track on the lower north-west slope of Knockastakeen. There is a stream a little to the left of the track and this meets up with a road. Walk down this road and turn right and walk back to the start.

Alternatively, from O'Loughlin's Castle, ascend east to Greenane and descend northeast to Farbreaga. From the summit, descend northwest to go back into the Muskry glen and meet up with the original path. If taking this shorter option then the *distance* will change to 10.5km, the *ascent* to 670 m and the *time* to 4.5 hrs.

ROUTE 7
CAHERBARNA BY GORTAVEHY – EAST GULLY

Distance: 7km   *Ascent*: 460m
Time: 4 hrs   *Terrain*: *Easy* to *Hard* scrambling, *Diff* climbing
Ref.: O.S. Map 79   *Start*: W205890
Equipment: 8mm or 9mm rope, slings and karabiners needed.

The Caherbarna group west of Millstreet is certainly worth con-
sidering. Though the top is featureless and very boggy, the north-
facing coums are spectacular and seldom visited. From Millstreet,
drive for 5km on the Rathmore road and turn left at Ballydaly
Cross Roads. Drive for 1.5km to Croohig's Cross Roads and turn
right. Drive a further 2.25km to the entrance of Gortavehy coum,
turn left and park off the dirt road near the entrance. Walk a little
southeast of the lake to the start of the obvious gully, which is
veering slightly north of east, between two main crags, the first
being over the lake and the second further southeast.

Walk up steep ground, staying on the left of the stream, to the
entrance of the gully, and cross a fence. Reach a short, wet slab
and climb *Easy* scrambling, to the right of this on steep and vegetated ground. Re-enter the gully, and a little further up reach
another wet slab and climb initially on the left, before traversing
to the right, halfway up, and continue on the right, with *Moderate*
scrambling. A short distance up, traverse to the left again and
climb on a grass ramp. This leads back into the gully. Intermittent
Easy to *Moderate* scrambling for a short distance will become a little more consistent as height is gained. Reach another fence and
at this point it is possible to leave the gully to the right. If continuing, the ground becomes *Hard* scrambling in wet conditions.
Continue to an awkward, *Diff* rockclimbing move, by climbing to
a wedged slab, and swinging around to the right of this, then up.
A little further on is a section of slab leading to overhanging rocks.
The overhang can be avoided by climbing to the right but the

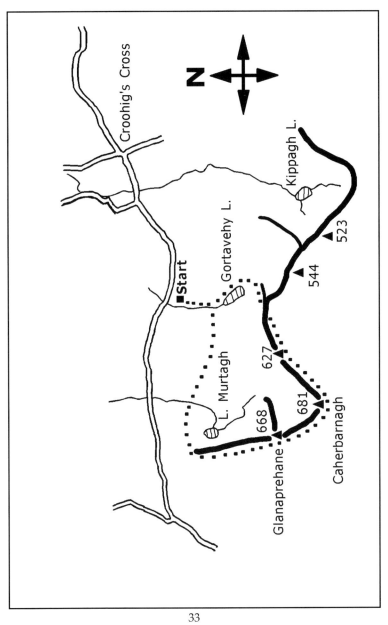

*The east-facing gully sweeping down to the
south-east corner of Gortavehy Lake.*

slabs are very wet and slippery so it is best to avoid this by making an *Easy* scramble move to the right before reaching the slabs. Re-enter the gully above this obstacle and continue to the top on intermittent *Easy* to *Moderate* scrambling.

Walk southwest, ascending gently to the summit cairn of Caherbarna. From here, change direction to the northwest and walk to the summit of Glanaprehane. Change direction, north-northwest and curve around the coum and walk down a long slope. Reach a fence but do not cross over. Turn right and follow a way-marked path east to Gortavehy and back to the start.

ROUTE 8
CAPPAGH EAST FACE

Distance: 8km   *Ascent*: 500m
Time: 4 hrs   *Terrain*: *Easy* to *Hard* scrambling
Ref.: O.S. Map 79   *Start*: W034840
Equipment: 8mm or 9mm rope, slings and karabiners needed.

This gorge-like glen is lush with oak, birch and holly, and the topography is a good example of ancient volcanic activity. Drive 1.5km past the village of Glenflesk on the N22 heading for Killarney. There is a turn-off on the left for Lough Guitane. Follow this road for just over 2km and turn left on a road which contours around Lough Guitane on its east side. Drive down this road for 2.5km as far as a bridge and park just off the road. Do not cross the bridge. Walk along an obvious track which leads into the glen.

The east side of Cappagh can only be described as adventurous. It is filled with crags, short ridges and gullies, rock slabs and general chaos. Climbing and scrambling options are numerous but should only be attempted on a dry day as a lot of the steep ground is a mixture of rock and grass. Turn into the glen from the north shoulder of Bennaunmore and walk for 800m before turning right and crossing the Cappagh river to ascend this rugged area. There is a gully high up on the right of a distinctive crag more or less under the height mark for Cappagh at 535m. On the way up there are many options to scramble and climb on, some being quite steep. Do not attempt to climb the gully as it is always wet and the crux move difficult and unprotected. To the right of the gully is steep ground with some exposed moves of *moderate* and *Hard* scrambling on relatively good rock. Again the choices are numerous and 50m to 60m of climbing will exit at the top of Cappagh. Descend southwest to the Cappagh river and follow it through a wooded gorge back to the glen. Keep to the east side of the river in the Cappagh glen as it is easier underfoot. Meet the

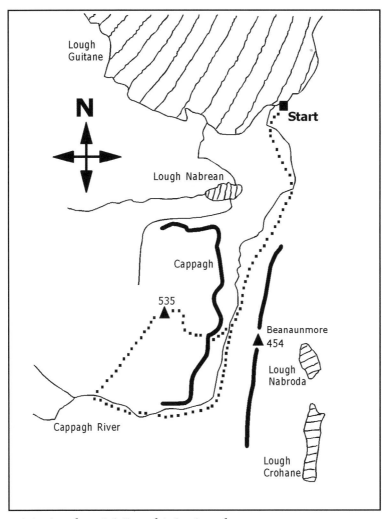

original path and follow this back to the start.

Though *distance* and *ascent* are short, the *time* can vary as there is such a variety of scrambling and climbing to choose from in this area.

The east face of Cappagh with its numerous scrambling and climbing options and the exit scramble to the right of the gully

ROUTE 9
KNOCKBOY BY AKINKEEN – NORTH-EAST GULLY

Distance: 9 km   *Ascent*: 650m
Time: 5 hrs   *Terrain*: *Easy* to *Hard* scrambling and two moves
                         of *V. Diff* rockclimbing
Ref.: O.S. Map 85   *Start*: W022657
Equipment: 8mm or 9mm rope, slings and karabiners needed.

Just outside the village of Kilgarvan heading for Kenmare on the R569, there is a left turn for Bantry. This road ascends to a pass between the Shehy and Caha Mountains. Drive up this road and after 7km pass through a tunnel. Another 2km further on there is a sharp bend at a bridge. Park the car off the road in the lay-by and do not obstruct the gate as it is the access to the forest plantation around Lough Akinkeen.

Walk up the track to the lake and walk around the lake, to the right rather than the left, as it is marginally easier. The crag is impressive, rising 350m above the lake and is north-northeast facing. The majority of it does not look climbable. The gully is on the right of the crag but not the one to the far right which is shorter and closer to the north-east ridge. There is a gully to its left which is very distinctive and does not look climbable. The lake is at 300m and the gully begins properly at 400m and rises for 200m. After some *Easy* scrambling at the start there is a grass ramp to the left which is a *Hard* scramble move. Shortly after this there is a vertical section of rock blocking the way so avoid this by climbing to the right of the gully which will present another vertical section of about 4m. The right corner of this is difficult so move to the left of it a little and climb this section with difficulty and no dignity. This could be taken as one of the *V. Diff* moves in the gully. Needless to say use a rope here, more for the second than the leader, as it cannot be protected. The gully is filled with *Moderate* scramble moves and a *Hard* scramble move three-quarters of the way up. Near the top, the gully branches into two, with the right

39

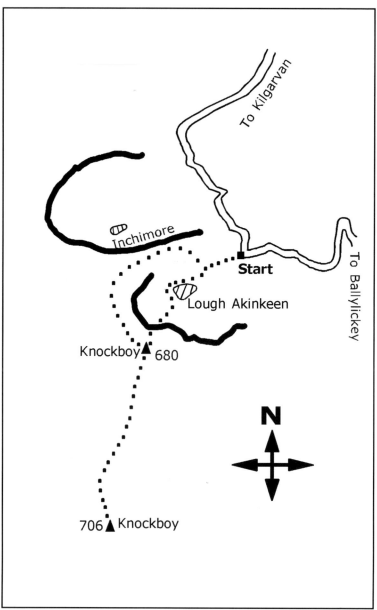

The right-trending, north-east gully above Lough Akinkeen with its two exit options at the top. It is the most logical ascent on this practically unclimbable face.

fork being the easier option. Continue up this but do not exit at the very top as it is messy and difficult. Instead move out to the right and leave the gully this way. If taking the left option, do not attempt the final vertical section. Instead there is a short, *V. Diff* move on the left which leads on to a grass ramp. Move to the top of this and climb over a 2m-section and though it is an *Easy* move and not high, it is an exposed spot so take nothing for granted. The summit cairn of Knockboy is close at a height of 680m, but this is not the main summit of Knockboy at 706m. To reach this head south-southwest for 2.5km. Return the same way to the cairn and descend by firstly heading northwest and then swinging north-northeast and then northeast around Lough Akinkeen. There is no need to go down the full ridge. Just beyond the lake, turn right and descend to the track. Follow this back to the start.

ROUTE 10
HUNGRY HILL BY COOMARKANE – EAST GULLY

Distance: 5.5km   *Ascent:* 600m
Time: 5 hrs.   *Terrain: Easy* to *Hard* scrambling, and up to *V.*
         Diff rockclimbing
Ref.: O.S Map 84   *Start:* V779493
Equipment: 9mm or 11mm rope, full range of rockclimbing equipment, harness, slings, helmet and karabiners needed.

From the turnoff for the Healy Pass, in the village of Adrigole, on the south side of the Beara Peninsula, drive for 1.5km on the R572 and take the second right turn. Ignore the first right turn, which has a signpost for Hungry Hill Waterfall.

Drive for 2km and park on the left. Go over a stile onto boggy ground and head west to meet the stream which flows from Coomarkane Lake. Follow the stream up to the lake which is situated under the east face of the south summit of Hungry Hill. Walk around to the north corner of the lake to the base of the gully on this section of the east face.

Begin to climb to the left of the gully, *Hard* scrambling and one move of *Diff* climbing on mixed grass and rock. Move back into the gully after this initial section and walk steep ground to a slab of rock. Go to the left of this obstacle, climbing a small buttress of rock, *Moderate* scramble move followed by a *Hard* scramble move over the slab to the right. Drop down a little to get back into the gully and move up to an obvious chimney. It is steeper and longer than it looks and is wet and vegetated. There are good hand holds on the rock on the right, *V. Diff* climbing. Shortly after this section, reach a short crag and climb on a left trending ramp of rock, *V. Diff* move to a grass platform. Make an awkward, short, *V. Diff* move out of this mainly on grass, with some handholds on the right. Proceed on steep ground to the next section, which is a short, *Hard* scramble move on the right and then an awkward *V. Diff* move to gain the gully again. The next obstacle,

43

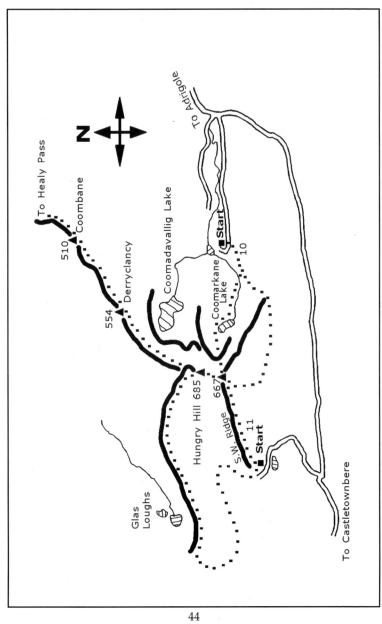

*The east face of the south peak of Hungry Hill, and the line
of ascent which starts at the north end of Coomarkane Lake.*

a short distance up, is an overhanging rock which should be avoided by *Hard* scrambling on steep ground, using the rock on the left to provide adequate hand-holds. Move back into the gully to the right and down a little. A short, *Hard* scramble move into a narrowing part of the gully leads to a crag. Go left and climb *Easy* to *Moderate* scrambling and reach another vertical crag. Go left again, and cross over a rock spine, dropping a little to steep ground. *Hard* scrambling, using the rock on the right for hand-holds, reaches a ramp. From here on up, follow the ramp, trending left until the top of a distinctive gully is met (and also a fence). Scramble on the rock on the right, *Easy* scrambling, and a short walk to the south summit. Descend south on steep, rocky ground to the 300m contour line approximately, and contour around the east spur as far as the Coomarkane stream. Follow this down, and back to the start.

ROUTE 11
HUNGRY HILL BY THE SOUTH-WEST RIDGE

Distance: 9km   *Ascent*: 600m
Time: 5 hrs   *Terrain*: A long ridge of *Easy* scrambling with many harder options
Ref.: O.S. Map 84   *Start*: V748484
Equipment: 8mm or 9mm rope, slings and karabiners needed.

From the turn-off for the Healy Pass, in the village of Adrigole on the south side of the Beara Peninsula, drive 7.5km on the R572 towards Castletownbere and turn right, off the main road. Drive up this road for 1km and park the car near Park Lough. Walk along the track for a couple of hundred metres and begin the ascent of the South-west Ridge immediately on leaving the track. The ridge is 1.5km long and rises to the south summit of Hungry Hill at 667m. All the *Hard* sections can be avoided so the ridge is graded as an *Easy* scramble but throughout the entire ridge, many options for harder scrambling and rockclimbing are available so it is an 'a la carte' type of day out, especially in dry conditions.

Move north-northeast from the south summit to get onto the north summit a short distance away. From here walk north for 500m before turning northwest and move along the county bounds for just over a half kilometre and change direction again. Move generally southwest to a height marked 442m. Navigation is difficult here as the ground is undulating and deceptive with no distinctive features to use. From here the two lakes named Glas Loughs should be visible to the northwest a couple of hundred metres away. The lakes feed the Glanmore river which flows northeast. Directly west and over 500m away is a bog road. Reach the road and descend this southwards for a kilometre and meet up with the O'Sullivan-Bere Way. Follow the Way east to Comnagapple glen and turn south to get back to the start.

If two cars are available then it is worth walking along the county bounds to the Healy Pass. To do this, walk northwards

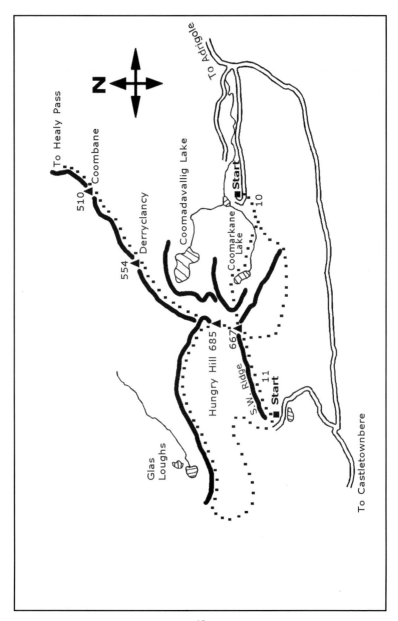

11

*The skyline from left to right is the
south-west ridge of Hungry Hill.*

from the north summit for 500m before turning northeast to get to the col between Derryclancy and Hungry Hill. Continue northeast to Coombane and about 600m further on change direction to walk north-northwest for another 500m before swinging right slightly to descend to the Healy Pass in a north-northeasterly direction.

This is an enjoyable line walk in good visibility but to be avoided if conditions are bad, as navigation is problematic with steep and dangerous ground east of Hungry Hill and on the Glanmore side between Derryclancy and Coombane. If taking this option then the *distance* will change to 7km, the *ascent* to 700m but the *time* remains generally the same.

It has to be emphasised that because of the numerous climbing options on the Southwest Ridge, the time given in the summary is very general and subject to change.

ROUTE 12
CARRAUNTOOHIL BY CUMMENAGEARAGH – NORTH-EAST GULLY

Distance: 12.5km   *Ascent:* 1080m
Time: 6.5 hrs   *Terrain*: Scot. I or II
Ref.: O.S. Map 78   *Start*: V826875
Equipment: 8mm or 9mm rope, crampons, ice axe, slings a karabiners needed.

The Macgillycuddy's Reeks is an impressive chain of mountains southwest of Killarney and contains most of Ireland's highest peaks. The area covers approximately 50 sq km and the chain runs for 15km from the Gap of Dunloe on the northeast to Lough Acoose on the west. Climbers and walkers flock to these mountains all year round as they offer some of the finest terrain in the country.

From Killarney take the Killorglin road, the R562, as far as Beaufort Bridge. Turn left, cross the bridge and drive as far as the crossroads. To go to Kate Kearney's cottage for The Gap of Dunloe, drive straight through for 1.5km. To go to Lisleibane for The Hag's Glen, turn right at the crossroads and drive for 5km past a shop and small petrol station and also a sign for Carrauntoohil. Do not take this left turn but instead turn left a little further on after a bridge and drive on a narrow road for 1km before taking the left fork shortly after another bridge and sharp turn in the road. Drive up this road, gaining some height, and after 1km park the car on the right. This area is known as Lisleibane and is the starting point for the Hag's Glen. *Keep the gates clear at all times as they are in constant use, especially by Kerry Mountain Rescue.*

Go through the left gate at Lisleibane, but instead of walking on the path, head directly for Knockbrinnea for 400m and then turn half-right to go in a southwesterly direction. It is 3km to

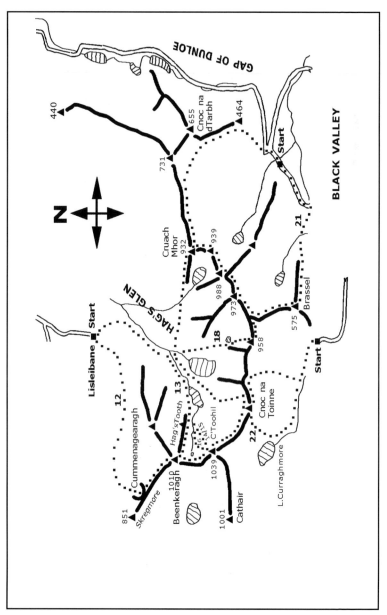

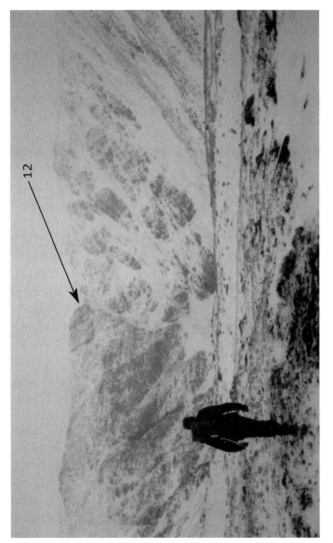

12

Cummenagearagh's north-east gully exiting on the ridge between Skregmore and Beenkeragh.

Cummenagearagh (not named in the 1:50,000 OS map) which is at an elevation of 560m. The gully is well defined at the back of the coum and depending on conditions it can vary from Scot I to Scot II. It is a straightforward climb with no complications and the best time to climb it is when the snow has consolidated in it over a period of cold weather (unfortunately not something that happens every year in the southwest). The gully exits on the Screig Mor/Beenkeeragh ridge at 830m. Ascend another 180m to get to the summit of Beenkeragh. From Beenkeragh, head southwest to get on the Beenkeragh/Carrauntoohil ridge and be careful here not to wander on to the Hag's Tooth ridge in bad visibility. The ridge is popular and has a well-defined path on its western side after the initial descent from Beenkeragh but it can be crossed by staying on the arête which is exposed and involves *Easy* to *Hard* scrambling. After 750m of ridge which is generally at Scot I in winter conditions, there is a final pull up to the summit of Carrauntoohil. Crossing the ridge reveals some of the finest mountain scenery in the country, with Coumloughra on the right, the Eagle's Nest on the left and the north faces of Caher and Carrauntoohil ahead. From the top of Carrauntoohil, move southeast to the col and the top of the Devil's Ladder but instead of descending here (it is in a very eroded condition) continue to the summit of Cnoc na Toinne. The top is level for about 500m and after walking for 300m northeast, turn north to descend via the poorly-defined grass, zig-zag path called Bóthar na Gaoithe, into the Hag's Glen. Care should be taken to avoid the dangerous ground of Eisc Cailli to the right and near the end of the descent, on the left for about the last 100m. Reach the path and walk back down the glen to Lisleibane. In good winter conditions this is a thoroughly enjoyable day out taking in a variety of mountain terrain. If unsure of descending by Cnoc na Toinne then use The Devil's Ladder as an escape route.

ROUTE 13
CARRAUNTOOHIL BY THE HAG'S TOOTH RIDGE

Distance: 12km   *Ascent*: 1060m
Time: 6 hrs   *Terrain*: A long ridge of *Easy* scrambling
Ref.: O.S. Map 78   *Start*: V826875
Equipment: 8 mm or 9 mm rope, slings and karabiners needed.

Start at Lisleibane and walk along the track into the Hag's Glen as far as the ford which is 2.5 km from the car park. At the ford, turn half-right and walk for a few minutes on level ground before ascending on to high ground over the north bank of Lough Gouragh.

OPTION 1: The easiest and safest way to approach the Tooth is to ascend the grassy gully on its right. The gully steepens to about 45 degrees and has a lot of loose rock and scree,and curves to the left, higher up to the base of the Tooth. Climb as far as the base and if the pinnacle is to be climbed there are some short, *Easy* to *Moderate* scramble moves on to it. Retreat back down the pinnacle the same way and staying on the north side, go around the pinnacle on a well worn path. A good rule of thumb is that the entire ridge can be climbed with nothing more difficult than *Easy* scrambling, and though there are numerous climbing options along this kilometre long ridge on short pinnacles, they should be avoided unless properly equipped for rockclimbing. It is a superb ridge with panoramic views of the 'Reeks' and especially the north and north-east faces of Carrauntoohil.

   The ridge finishes on the summit of Beenkeragh and if a shorter day is preferred then descend by Knockbrinnea which will change the *distance* to 8 km, the *ascent* to 880m and the *time* to 4.5 hrs. To do this head northeast for Knockbrinnea's west peak at 854m and continue northeast to Lisleibane. The initial part of this descent is a boulder field and it can be difficult and a

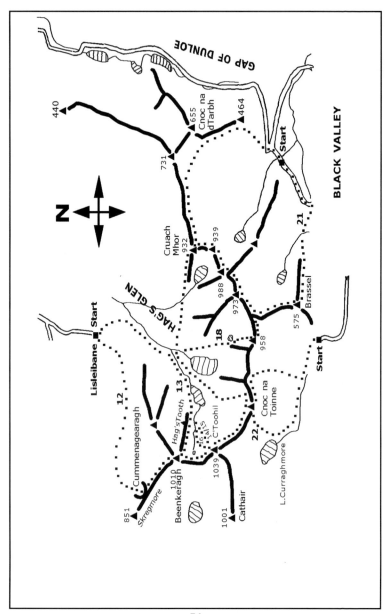

*The imposing Hag's Tooth with the easier option following
the grassy gully to its right and the harder,
more direct approach up the face.*

little dangerous if careless or tired. If continuing to Carrauntoohil and Cnoc na Toinne then proceed as described in Route 12.

OPTION 2: This involves a direct climb of the Hag's Tooth ridge. The approach is identical except do not ascend the grass gully on the right. Walk a little beyond where the path meets the gully, above the cliffs over Lough Gouragh. There are various options to choose from to begin, and the most accessible is to the right of a cut or short gully, in the middle of the rock formation.

Hard scrambling and *Moderate* rockclimbing, trending right of the cut, arrives at a wide platform after about 15m. Climb approximately 5m of rock slabs with no protection, *V. Diff* climbing, to a grass ledge, right of an obvious overhang. *Diff* move leads out of this, with good protection onto steep ground and mixed scrambling on short rock sections to the Tooth. It is possible to walk off the ridge and into the gully on the right at various points on the ascent to the Tooth.

On the final section of the Tooth it is safer and easier to stay on the left. A short, *Diff* move leads onto the ridge, followed by some mixed scrambling and another two moves of *Diff* climbing before mixed scrambling to the top of the Tooth. Proceed as already described.

ROUTE 14
CARROUNTOOHIL BY HOWLING RIDGE

Distance: 9.5km   *Ascent*: 980m
Time: 6 hrs   *Terrain*: *Easy* to *Hard* scrambling. Several pitches
                          of *V. Diff* rockclimbling
Ref.: O.S. Map 78   *Start*: V826875
Equipment: 11mm rope, slings, karabiners, climbing harness, rockclimb-ing equipment and helmet.

Howling Ridge is one of the classic mountaineering routes in Ireland. It is a mixture of scrambling and *V. Diff* rockclimbing pitches and is a popular ridge, climbed by many, so a lot of the loose rock has been knocked off, but the golden rule always applies: 'test everything before making a commitment' as there is always loose rock on this route. It is on the north-east face of Carrauntoohil and is dramatic and exposed in places. The gully on its left is Collins' Gully and the formidable Primrose Ridge on its right meets Howling Ridge near the top.

Start at Lisleibane and walk to the ford. Follow the same route for the Hag's Tooth but keep to the path and ascend to the first Level to the south of the Tooth. Do not go up to the second level but ascend to the platform southwards. Continue south to an obvious gully and ascend the gully to the feature known as the 'Heavenly Gates'. This is the starting point for the climb. Route finding is straightforward enough and though a full rack of climbing equipment should be taken, I find that placement is sparse enough though slings are used a lot throughout the climb. It should be noted also that this is climbed as a summer route and if climbing in winter conditions (ie, show and ice) then the nature of the route changes and inevitably it becomes a far more serious undertaking.

Begin climbing immediately from the 'Heavenly Gates' on to consistent *Hard* scrambling with one short move of *Diff* rock-climbing. Approximately 40m of climbing will reach the first rock

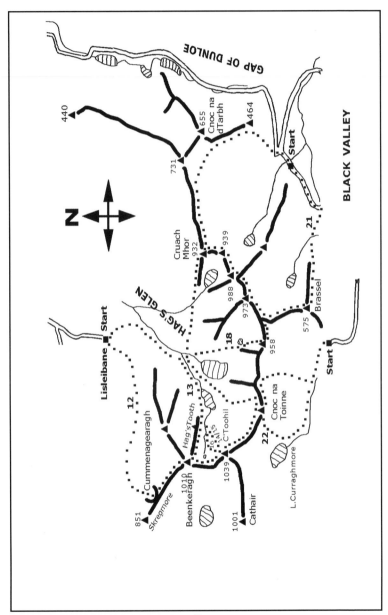

The north-east face of Carrauntoohil, with Pipet's Ridge (15) on the skyline and Howling Ridge (14), beside it, to the right.

step which is *V. Diff* for the first 5m and then mixed scrambling to the next obvious step. It is also *V. Diff* and the difficulty is on the initial 4m of climbing. Consistent *Hard* scrambling leads to the next difficulty which is short but awkward as the stratification is slanting diagonally, down to the left. This delicate *V. Diff* move is followed by *Hard* scrambling to the next feature which is known by some as the 'Finger'. Climb *Diff* to the top, and traverse to the left leading to *Diff* climbing on exposed ridge above Collins' Gully. This leads to a short, dramatic knife-edge ridge near the top of the climb but it is just a careful walk with nothing technical to contend with.

There is only one section to climb to complete the ridge and two options present themselves: to continue with the ridge or to go into Collins' Gully on the left and climb out of this. The latter is much safer and the exit move can be protected. This is my preference as the final section of the ridge is very loose and badly protected. After this, there are two, short moves of *Diff* climbing and then the final 100m of just steep ground to the summit of Carrauntoohil. From here descend northwest to the Beenkeragh Ridge and then northwards to Beenkeragh. If scrambling options are to be maximised then leave the path and stick to the arête as it offers some of the finest scrambling in the country.

From the summit of Beenkeragh head northeast to Knockbrinnea and continue northeast to Lisleibane on what seems like a never-ending slope. An alternative descent is to go down to the col from Carrauntoohil to get on to the Beenkeragh Ridge and descend O'Shea's Gully. This will descend to the upper level and the small lake known as the Devil's Looking Glass. Follow the levels down and pick up the path originally used to get on to the first level. If taking this slightly shorter option then the *distance* will change to 7km, the *ascent* to 880m and the *time* to 5 hrs, 20 mins.

ROUTE 15
CARRAUNTOOHIL BY PIPET'S RIDGE

Distance: 11km   *Ascent*: 994m
Time: 6 hrs   *Terrain*: *Easy* to *Hard* scrambling with one section
                         of *Severe* rockclimbing.
Ref.: O.S. Map 78   *Start*: V826875
Equipment: 9mm or 11mm rope, slings, karabiners, climbing harness, rockclimbing equipment and helmet needed.

The approach is identical to that of Howling Ridge. From the Heavenly Gates, cross the stream coming out of Collins' Gully and walk to the high point of the path. The path levels off and after walking along this for several more metres, turn right to ascend steep grassy ground. Stay away from the complicated ground on the right of the ridge initially and approach the obvious buttress at an oblique angle from the left using the shallow gully on the left as a point of reference. Move to an obvious rock pinnacle at the base of the buttress and climb between it and the buttress. Make a short *Hard* scramble move out of this and follow a ramp trending to the right. Get off the ramp to the left onto a broad grassy slope. Belay the Second from here before moving onto the next section. There is a crag directly in front. Avoid this by moving to the left and making an awkward, *Hard* scramble move over this short wall. Continue on steep ground, keeping to the right, and move up to the only difficult obstacle on the ridge which is a wall approximately 4m high, graded at *Severe* rockclimbing and well protected. After this the ridge comprises of consistent, mixed scrambling with magnificent views of its neighbouring, Howling Ridge on the right. The ridge peters out approximately 150m from the summit of Carrauntoohil.

The summary is calculated for descending by Cnoc na Toinne. If carrying on to Beenkeragh then refer to the description for Howling Ridge Route 14.

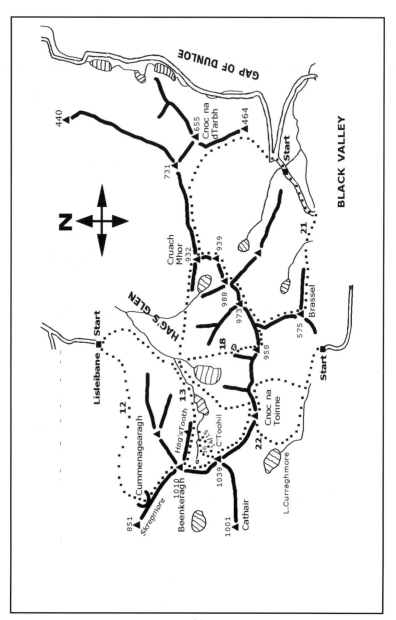

*The north-east face of Carrauntoohil, with Pipet's Ridge
(15) on the skyline and Howling Ridge (14),
beside it, to the right.*

ROUTE 16
CARRAUNTOOHIL BY CURVED GULLY RIDGE

Distance: 11.5km *Ascent:* 994m
Time: 8 hrs *Terrain: Easy* to *Hard* scrambling, *Diff* to *Hard Severe* rockclimbing.
Ref.: O.S. Map 78 *Start*: V826875
Equipment: 2 x 9mm rope, full range of rockclimbing equipment, slings, helmet and harness needed.

I have called this Curved Gully Ridge, which is a bit contradictory but it does describe the location of the ridge adequately. This ridge makes up the west wall of Curved Gully, a well-known route up to the summit of Carrauntoohil and follows the same line as the gully.

From Lisleibane, follow the route for Howling Ridge as far as the First Level, south of the Hag's Tooth. Move west on to the second level either by staying right of the waterfall on the east facing crag or by going over to the left and using a well-worn path there. Right of the waterfall can be a bit wet in places and there will be the occasional *Easy* scramble move, and if taking the left option there is a lot of loose scree on the path which can be a bit annoying.

Instead of going onto the third level by the normal route, stay left and walk to the start of Curved Gully. Some *Hard* scrambling on this initial section of the gully emerges onto more open ground where the gully becomes shallow. Leave the gully and walk on its right, up to the base of the ridge, overlooking the gully for the most part.

The first pitch poses no great difficulties, except for a short section of *V. Diff* climbing near the start. This can be well protected. From here it is just mixed scrambling to an obvious belay position after a run out of 40m of rope. The second pitch has a *V. Diff* slightly overhanging start which leads on to mixed scrambling until a final 4m to 5m of vertical *Severe* climbing to the next belay position and almost a full rope length. It is important to stay left

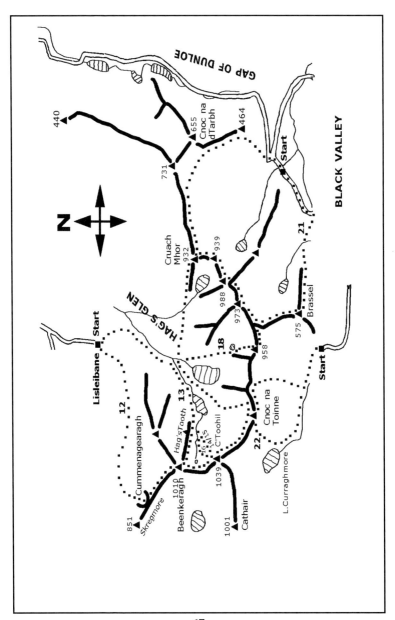

The well-defined west wall of Curved Gully, starting on the Second Level, provides an excellent mountaineering route to the summit of Carrauntoohil.

here close to the gully and the move can be protected. The third pitch is the hardest. An exposed move of *Hard Severe* climbing on the left to exit the belay position, mixed scrambling and some *V. Diff* climbing to a final vertical section of between 4m to 6m high, *Hard Severe* climbing, which can be protected. This pitch is a full rope length and has an excellent belay stance. From here it is mixed scrambling leading to a track and quickly to the summit of Carrauntoohil.

The summary is calculated for a descent by Cnoc na Toinne. If carrying on to Beenkeragh then refer to the description for Howling Ridge, Route 14. Alternatively descend O'Shea's Gully and down the three levels, which will change the *distance* to 10km, the *ascent* to 874m and the *time* to 7 hrs 20mins.

ROUTE 17
CAHER BY LOUGH EAGHER – NORTH-EAST RIDGE

Distance: 9.5km   *Ascent*: 750m
Time: 6.5 hrs   *Terrain*: *Easy* to *Hard* scrambling, *Diff* to *V. Diff*
                         climbing
Ref.: O.S. Map 78   *Start*: V771871
Equipment: 9mm or 11mm rope, full range of rockclimbing equipment,
climbing harness, helmet, slings and karabiners needed

Lough Acoose is situated 11km directly south of Killorglin and
using this as a reference point, drive 1.5km northeast to the start
of this route. It is not permitted to park in front of the wooden
gate, which is the entrance to the hydro-dam at the outflow of the
lakes. A couple of hundred metres further up the road is a suitable
area for parking, on the right. Walk back to the start and cross
over the wooden gate and walk up a steep, concrete road to the
coum and the first of the three lakes, Lough Eighter. Walk on the
left side of the first two lakes, and then cross to the right side
between Lough Coomloughra and Lough Eagher.

The ridge is not obvious at first, and can easily be mistaken
for another, more distinctive ridge to its right. Walk around to the
south-east corner of Lough Eagher and ascend steep, boulder-
strewn ground, following a curving, shallow stream to an obvious
crag. This is the start of the ridge and is approximately at the
550m contour line, 80m above the lake.

Begin to climb, staying on the right of the gully in the middle
of this crag; *Diff* climbing at first, followed by mixed scrambling.
Enter the gully after some height is gained and belay from an
obvious stance where the gully ends. Exit the gully to the left and
staying on the left, walk on steep ground, over a gully which runs
parallel with the ridge all the way to the top. The ground soon
becomes mixed, consistent scrambling on relatively good rock. It
is necessary to pitch some short sections of *V. Diff* climbing higher up, and though several of the key moves are on a mixture of

Route 17

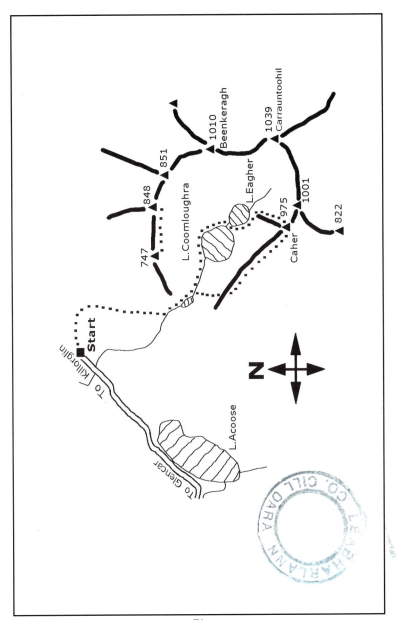

The north-east ridge starts just above the southeast end of Lough Eagher and, though not immediately obvious on approach, is well worth the effort.

grass and rock, with some exposure, they can be adequately protected (but it is important not to do this ridge in wet conditions). The rock becomes more broken as height is gained.

Near the top, the ridge dissipates and meets the paralleling gully on the left. Move right and scramble up steep grass towards an obvious crag and climb some *Hard* scrambling up a short but awkward gully bisecting the crag. Exit the gully to the left and *Easy* scrambling becomes just steep ground, exiting west of the western summit of Caher at about 850m.

Descending is straightforward, following the north-west ridge above the lakes. Come off the ridge after 1.5km and descend northwards to Lough Eighter, to walk back down the road to the start.

ROUTE 18
CRUACH MHÓR BY CUMMEENMORE – NORTH-EAST GULLY

Distance: 12km   *Ascent*: 1058m
Time: 6 hrs   *Terrain: Easy* to *Hard* scrambling.
Ref.: O.S. Map 78   *Start*: V826875
Equipment: 8mm or 9mm rope, slings and karabiners needed.

Start at Lisleibane and walk into the Hag's Glen as far as the ford. A little beyond the ford at Lough Callee leave the path to the left and contour around the lake on its eastern side before ascending to high ground, changing direction southeast. Follow a stream into Cummeenmore, staying on high ground above the lake to the right.

OPTION 1: There is an obvious gully on the right hand side of the coum. Climb on the left bank of the gully initially before crossing to the right on reaching the waterfall. Avoid this by climbing out to the right, *Easy* to *Moderate* scrambling. Enter the gully again and climb up to another waterfall. Climb to the left to bypass this. Walk on less steep ground to the start of the next section of the gully, ignoring the right fork. The ground begins to steepen again to meet the next obstacle, which is a section of large, wet, and overgrown boulders. An initial *Moderate* scramble move is followed by a short, *Hard* move to complete this section.

Continue up to meet another, steep section of roughly 6m high. Staying on the line of the stream, though wet, is the safest and easiest option. The top section of this is very loose so great care must be taken. Nothing on this section exceeds *Moderate* to *Hard* scrambling.

Beyond this it is just a walk to the top on open ground. Exit onto the ridge, on the east side of Cnoc an Chuillinn, 30m below the summit.

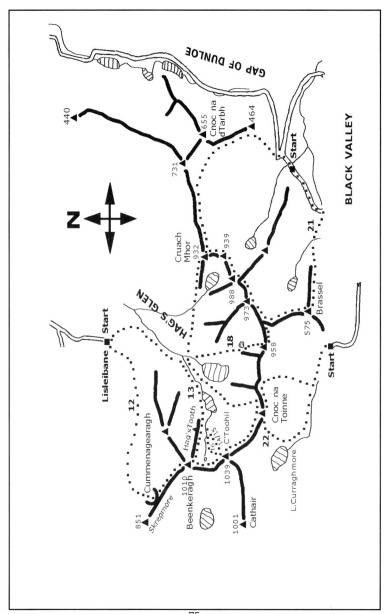

Cummeenmore coum on the north side of Cnoc an Chuillinn and the distinctive north-east ridge.

OPTION 2: Approach Cummeenmore the same way and on reaching the high ground to the right (west) of the lake, continue up the north-east ridge. Basically it is no more difficult than intermittent *Easy* scrambling though harder options can be attempted but I do not recommend it as the ground is a mixture of grass and broken rock. This approach to Cnoc an Chuillin does provide spectacular views, especially of the coum below, and gives a sense of exposure without the danger. The ridge meets the path, west of the summit and several metres below.

From Cnoc an Chuillinn, walk northeast to An Maolán Búi, and continue to Cnoc na Peasta northeast (the top of the Bone) and then north for the final section to the summit. Descend northeast to the col, and then turn north to reach the Big Gun. The path is well defined but my preference is to stick to the ridge, which provides consistent *Easy* to *Moderate* scrambling. Descend the Big Gun, moving north, and where the path drops a couple of metres and curves to the right, stay on the path for this section as backclimbing the pinnacle on the other side is dangerous and not recommended. After this, the ridge can be adhered to without interruption.

From Cruach Mhór, descend west on the boulder slope to Lough Cummeenapeasta and continue to descend west crossing the Gaddagh river, back to the Ford. It is easier to cross the Gaddagh River closer to Lough Callee rather than further downstream. Follow the track north, back to the start.

ROUTE 19
CNOC NA DTARBH BY THE NORTH-EAST SPUR

Distance: 10 km   *Ascent:* 746 m
Time: 4.5 hrs.   *Terrain*: *Easy* to *Hard* scrambling
Ref.: O.S. Map 78   *Start*: V880887
Equipment: 8mm or 9mm rope, slings and karabinersmay be needed.

From Kate Kearney's Cottage walk 2.5km south, through the Gap of Dunloe to a point on the road between Gushvally and Auger lakes.

Cross the River Loe and after a short distance reach the start of the ridge.

OPTION 1: The ridge can be divided into two parts: the first section is a series of steps, while the second is a steep slope to the top. The lower part of the first section tends to be wet but as height is gained the ground becomes drier and has more exposed rock.

Starting off, there is a wet step of 5m to 8m with one *Hard* scramble move.

After this ascend quickly on steep ground and some *Easy* scrambling to a short crag. Contour to the left of this to avoid any rockclimbing. Reach another short crag a little further up and stay on the left side of it also. Scrambling is mixed on short sections. The last portion of the ridge steepens and options on scrambling are available. There is nothing complicated or too difficult, though the ground is a little more exposed than already experienced.

OPTION 2: Start as for the first option and after completing the first section, there is a harder option to complete the ridge. Move to the left to an obvious gully on the right of a rock ridge. Scramble on the left of the gully to the first obstacle which is a short vertical section of approximately 5m and the move is equivalent to *Diff*

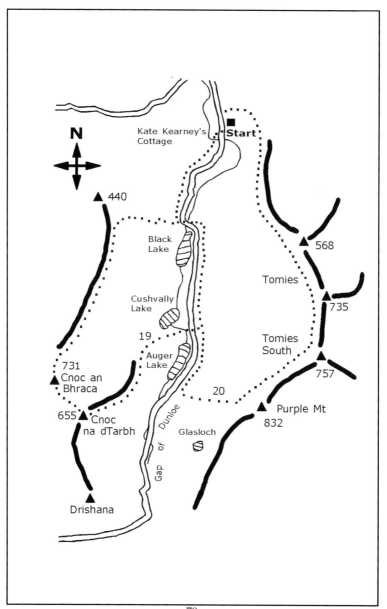

N

Kate Kearney's
Cottage

Start

▲ 440

Black
Lake

568

Tomies

Cushvally
Lake

735

19

Tomies
South

Auger
Lake

731
▲
Cnoc an
Bhraca

20

757

655 ▲
Cnoc
na dTarbh

Purple Mt
832

Gap of Dunloe

Glasloch

▲
Drishana

The north-east spur of Cnoc na dTarbh which starts at the north end of Auger Lake in the Gap of Dunloe.

rockclimbing in very wet conditions. There is a good belay position to bring up the Second. From here climb to the left on grass
and then back into the gully. A little further on there is another
obstacle of rock blocking the gully. Climb to the right on a *Hard*
scramble move made more difficult on wet and unstable ground.

The next section is at an angle of 45 degrees approximately, on
loose and wet ground. Reach an overhanging rock and exit to the
right, removing rucksacks to do so. The next 15m is very wet and
slimy on the right, though the wall on the left is dry and provides
enough handholds to complete this portion. Rucksacks tend to get
in the way in this narrow and restrictive space but they cannot be
removed. The final 15m of the gully can be avoided by exiting to
the right and completing the ridge on steep ground. If completing
the gully, avoid the final, direct move and climb the slab on the
right wall. This is wet but safe as it provides plenty of foot- and
hand-holds to complete the short move and a very good piece of
protection can be placed on the left wall higher than the slab. After
this, the gully peters out quickly to just steep ground to the top.

The summit of Cnoc na dTarbh is a further 700m away to the
southwest. From there change direction northwest to get on to
Cnoc an Bhráca. Descend northeastwards over a long, boggy section to meet the track, which zigzags back to the Gap of Dunloe
road near the car park.

ROUTE 20
PURPLE MOUNTAIN BY TURNPIKE ROCK

Distance: 10km   *Ascent*: 874m
Time: 5.5hrs   *Terrain: Easy* to *Hard* scrambling
Ref.: O.S. Map 78   *Start*: V88O887
Equipment: 8mm or 9mm rope, slings and karabiners needed.

From Kate Kearney's Cottage walk 3.5km into the Gap of Dunloe. Reach a bridge past Auger Lake where the road narrows and begins to ascend. Leave the road to the left before crossing the bridge. Elevation at this point is 150m. Begin climbing immediately. This west face of Purple Mountain provides mixed and consistent scrambling on short, rock steps with harder options if preferred. Route finding is simple as it is just a case of climbing eastwards towards the western summit of Purple Mountain.

The scrambling peters out at about an elevation of 550m. From the western summit, walk northeast for the main summit at 832m.

Continue northeast to the col and the summit of Tomies South. Change direction to the north to a col and then north-northeast for Tomies. Descend northwest to Gortadirra and then north down a long, heather slope to reach a dirt road. Turn left and walk back to the main road. On reaching this, turn left and walk a short distance back to the car park at Kate Kearney's Cottage.

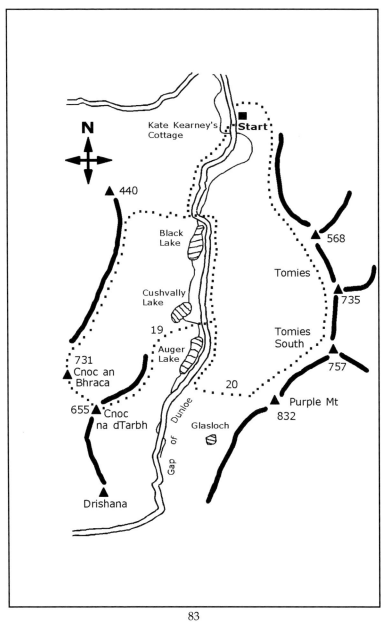

Kate Kearney's
Cottage

Start

N

440

Black
Lake

Tomies

568

735

Cushvally
Lake

19

Tomies
South

Auger
Lake

757

731
Cnoc an
Bhraca

20

Purple Mt

655 Cnoc
na dTarbh

832

Glasloch

Drishana

Turnpike Rock, in the Gap of Dunloe, provides numerous scrambling options on the western side of Purple Mountain.

ROUTE 21
CRUACH MHÓR BY BRASSEL EAST RIDGE

Distance: 11km   *Ascent:* 1080m
Time: 7.5 hrs   *Terrain*: *Easy* to *Hard* scrambling
Ref.: O.S. Map 78   *Start*: V855825
Equipment: 8mm or 9mm rope, slings and karabiners needed.

From Kate Kearney's Cottage drive into the Black Valley through the Gap of Dunloe. At the end of this road turn right and, after approximately 500m, park the car on the right, on some open ground next to a house. Walk southwest into the valley and 500m past the turn-off on the left (this road curves south of the two lakes), leave the road and turn right, heading to the foot of the east ridge of Brassel. Keep to the left of the river which flows southeast from Lough Callee (Lough Chuillean on the 1:25,000 scale map).

On reaching the base of the ridge, many options will present themselves, taking in mixed, consistent scrambling and harder if preferred. The ridge starts properly at the 250m contour and finishes at 450m, providing 200m of good scrambling. Three-quarters of the way up it is necessary to bypass a crag and going to the far left provides good scrambling on slabs with some exposure, on relatively good rock.

After the summit of Brassel at 575m, there is a long slope to the ridge between Cnoc an Chuillinn on the left and An Maolán Búi (the top of the bone) on the right. Walk northeast to An Maolán Búi and continue in generally the same direction to Cnoc na Peasta. Descend northeast to the col, and then turn north to reach the Big Gun. The path is well defined but my preference is to stick to the ridge which maximises scrambling options (*Easy* to *Moderate* scrambling). Descend the Big Gun, moving north.

Where the path drops a couple of metres and curves around a pinnacle to the right, stay on the path here as backclimbing the

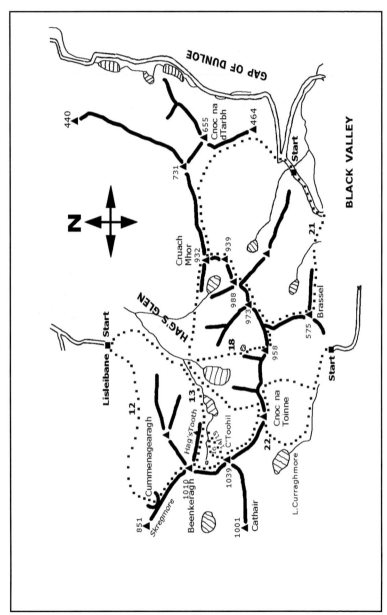

The east ridge of Brassel Mountain from the Black Valley gives an alternative approach to the eastern Reeks.

pinnacle on the other side is dangerous and not recommended. After this, the ridge can be adhered to without interruption.

From Cruach Mhór, descend northeast to the col and contour to Drishana, bypassing Cnoc na dTarbh. Descend southwest to the road and walk into the Black Valley, turning right and back to the start a short distance from the junction. An alternative descent is to go down the Feabrahy ridge from Cnoc na Peasta which would shorten the *distance* to 8km, the *ascent* to 957m and the *time* to 6 hrs.

ROUTE 22
CNOC NA TOINNE BY CURRAGHMORE – THE SOUTH-WEST GULLY

Distance: 5.5 km   *Ascent:* 720m
Time: 5.5 hrs.   *Terrain:* Mixed scrambling, *Diff* to *V. Diff* rock
                                 climbing
Ref.: O.S. MAP 78   *Srart*: V821820
Equipment: 9mm or 11mm rope, full range of rockclimbing equipment,
slings, helmet and harness needed.

Just over 2km west of the youth hostel in the Black Valley, turn left
and drive for 5km. Park opposite a shed in a little lay-by on the
right. Walk along the road, through a gate and reach another gate
and a group of houses. Bypass the houses by following the way-
marked path, which is part of the Kerry Way.

Go over a stile and cross two streams. Follow the stream to its
source, which is Curraghmore Lake. Reach the lake and look to
the right at the south-west face and the first distinctive gully on
the south-east end of the lake.

Cross the mouth of the stream and walk a short distance to
the start of the gully. Initially there is some *Easy* scrambling,
sometimes having to leave the gully either to the right or left. The
first difficulty is a section 4m high, wet and broken. Climb to the
left, *Moderate* to *Diff* climbing. Another *Hard* scramble move follows this shortly after, and is about 3m high and left or right is
equally difficult. Alternatively, stay on the buttress which bisects
the stream and climb this short *Hard* scramble section. A little further up, another *Hard* scramble move presents itself and it is best
to stay on the left, as the rock is relatively drier. This goes around
a very large boulder and leads on to a grass ramp.

Further up, at this stage approximately halfway up the gully,
are huge boulders blocking the way. Climb to the left, into a cave
and exit the cave using a choice of two escapes: one at the back
and one on the left, *Easy* to *Moderate* scramble moves. The next

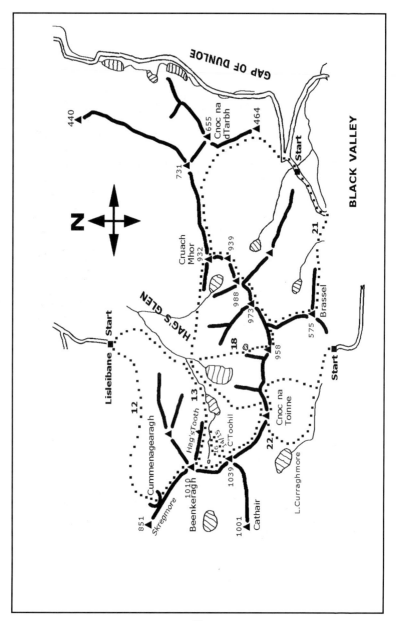

*The south-west gully below Croc na Toinne, as seen
from the southeastern end of Curraghmore Lake.*

obstacle, by far the hardest and most serious in the entire climb, is just a little further up after some *Easy* scrambling. This section is between 4m and 5m high and has to be climbed directly into a small waterfall. The walls on both sides of the gully are very steep and wet here so it cannot be avoided. Climb to a small ledge and exit to the right on steep grass and broken rock. A *caveat* has to be issued here.

Climb on steep ground to the next most difficult section which fortunately is not in the path of the stream. Climb on the right, onto a dry rock ramp, *V. Diff* move, which leads to steep and mixed rock and grass. This is awkward near the top with little or no firm foot- or hand-holds. The next block should be by-passed by climbing to the right, to a rock slab, staying on the right edge of the slab which is no more than *Moderate* or *Hard* scrambling. Mixed grass and rock follows, *Easy* to *Moderate* scrambling and the option now is to swing back into the gully which at this stage has become shallow, or just stay on the steep ground to the right which is no more than intermittent *Easy* scrambling for a while and then just steep ground to the top of Cnoc na Toinne.

Walk northeast for a couple of hundred meters before changing direction and descending southeast to the col. Change direction again to the south and descend steep ground, following the line of a fence which should be on the right and runs most of the way down to the road. Do not drift to the left to avoid the crags. Reach the road, turn left and walk a short distance back to the start.

ROUTE 23
COOMASAHARN HORSESHOE BY COOMACULLEN – NORTH RAMP

Distance: 9km   *Ascent:* 650m
Time: 5 hrs.   *Terrain:* *Easy* to *Hard* scrambling and *Diff*
                           climbing
Ref.: O.S. Map 78   *Start:* V637852
Equipment: 9mm or 11mm rope, slings and karabiners needed.

Drive into the village of Glenbeigh and turn left at the Towers Hotel. After driving for 7km, park off the road in the grass margin where the road turns sharply right. Follow a dirt road in towards the glen and reach a gate. Go through the gate and follow a vague track along the east side of the lake. Walk for 2km along the lake, and encounter an area of large boulders. To avoid a descent, it is necessary to make a short, *Hard* scramble move, using an obvious spike of rock to climb above this obstacle. Follow a track, dropping a little before reaching the waterfall which is the outflow from Coomacullen.

Staying on the left, walk up steep, boulder-strewn ground to the hanging valley of Coomacullen. There is a deep gully on the right of the north face and a buttress on its left. To the left of the buttress is an obvious ramp. It looks deceptively *Easy* but be warned in advance; it is consistent mixed scrambling, on ground which becomes steeper and more exposed as height is gained. Walk to the base and scramble up a stream on relatively good rock with plenty of hand- and foot-holds. As one gains height, the rock becomes less accommodating, with stratification becoming more angled and the rock more broken and wet. The right is more difficult than the left.

Near the top, it is necessary to traverse the stream to the left. Gain as much height as possible before making the move, and though the stream is very wet, the rock in it is solid. Great care

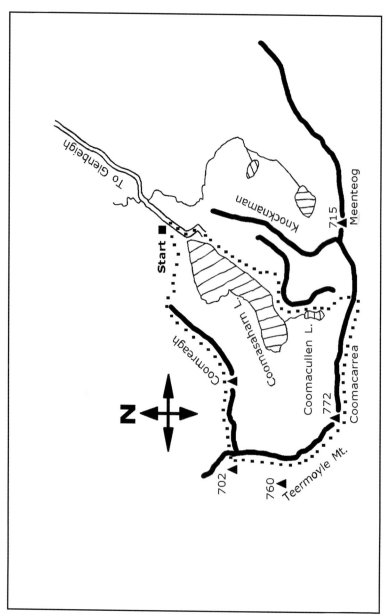

*The deceptively easy looking north ramp
above Coomacullen Lake.*

should be taken here as it is very exposed and a bit unnerving. Needless to say, a rope should be used. After the traverse, a *Moderate* scramble move will exit the left side of the stream and *Easy* to *Moderate* scrambling to the top. Exit to the west of Meentog.

Continue west to Coomacarrea and change direction northwest to reach the summit of Teermoyle Mountain. If visibility is poor, great care should be taken to get on to the arête to descend by Coomreagh. Walk northeast to the spot height 702 which is just over 750m away and change direction east-northeast to walk on to the arête. Though steep and narrow, it is still mainly a walk with an occasional *Easy* scramble move. Descend to the broader ridge of Coomreagh and change direction to the northeast. Reach a track which leads to the road and descend a short distance to the start.

ROUTE 24
COOMLOUGHRA NORTH-EAST GULLY – CLOON LAKE GLEN

Distance: 6.5km   *Ascent:* 500m
Time: 4.5 hrs   *Terrain: Easy* to *Hard* scrambling
Ref.: O.S. Map 79   *Start*: V704771
Equipment: 8mm or 9mm rope, slings and karabiners needed.

Travelling southwest from Glencar, take the first left after passing the Climber's Inn and drive for nearly 3km before turning right at the signpost for the Ballaghbeama Gap. After less than 1km, turn right for the Cloon Lake glen and drive for 4.5km, staying on the east side of the lake. Park at a junction where a road leads to a boathouse by the lake. Walk up the road, passing between two farmhouses and where the road turns sharply left to go up to a house higher up, leave the road and walk by a large stone wall. Cross a fence and follow an inconsistent path, running along the east side and a little above Lough Reagh. Cross another fence and encounter old stone walls, surrounding small fields and the remnants of 'cultivation ridges' – evidence of a larger population in the glen before the Famine.

Cross a boulder field and gradually angle down to the level of the lake and around to its south bank. Ascend a little and cross over a boggy area, staying to the right of an obvious hill at the back of the glen, heading southwest. Enter a narrow, oak-filled glen, and negotiate the wood to the base of an obvious gully (the left of two). There is nothing much of note in the gully for the first half, and then two short sections of *Hard* scrambling close together, staying to the right. *Easy* to *Moderate* scrambling to the next section near the top where several large boulders form a cave. Move to the back of the cave and climb through a narrow opening, *Moderate* but awkward move out. Rucksacks have to be removed to do this. Continue on the right and encounter several *Hard* scramble moves, staying on the right. After this, there is

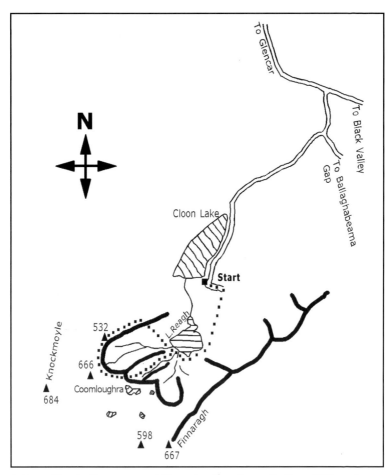

intermittent *Easy* scrambling to the top. Exit a little above Coomloughra. Turn right at the top and climb *Easy* scrambling on good slabs. Continue to the 600m contour line, which effectively is the top of a north-east ridge.

Descend this ridge, and though it is steep in places, it is a straightforward descent to Lough Reagh. Cross the boggy ground to the south bank of the lake and retrace the way back to the start.

The north-east gully, below Coomloughra, at the back of Lough Reagh in the Cloon Lake Glen.

ROUTE 25
KNOCKNAGANTEE – EAST RIDGE

Distance: 6km   *Ascent:* 570m
Time: 3.5 hrs   *Terrain: Easy* to *Hard* scrambling
Ref.: O.S. Map 78   *Start:* V669711
Equipment: 8mm or 9mm rope, slings and karabiners needed.

Driving from Kenmare on the N70, enter Sneem and cross a bridge. Turn right at the village green and then right again. Drive to a sign which says 'Cul de sac' and turn sharply to the left. Reach a fork and take the left. Drive for 5km up this road, ignoring any junctions, and reach another fork, continuing on the left. Cross over a bridge, and park on the left before reaching farm buildings a short distance away. Walk to the buildings, turn right and ascend the gravel road for less than a kilometre, before leaving the road to the right.

Walk northeastwards, crossing a bog, to Eagle's Lake at the base of the south-east-facing wall of Knocknagantee. Walk anticlockwise around the lake, crossing a stream, as far as the waterfall. Staying on the right of the falls, walk up steep ground with the occasional *Easy* scramble move. Reach slabs nearing the top, and scramble *Easy* to *Moderate* moves with occasional *Hard* scrambling.

Reach the smaller lake of Coomanassig at the base of the east ridge. Though the ridge is only 100m high, it provides excellent scrambling, with some serious exposure. It is necessary to have dry conditions to get the best out of this route, but if not, trend right to less exposed ground. Navigation is simple and the ridge finishes at about the 600m contour line.

Walk southwestwards for 700m to the summit cairn of Knocknagantee, staying on the right of the fence. From the summit, descend southwestwards and meet the gravel road originally taken at the start, though higher up. Descend the road back to the start.

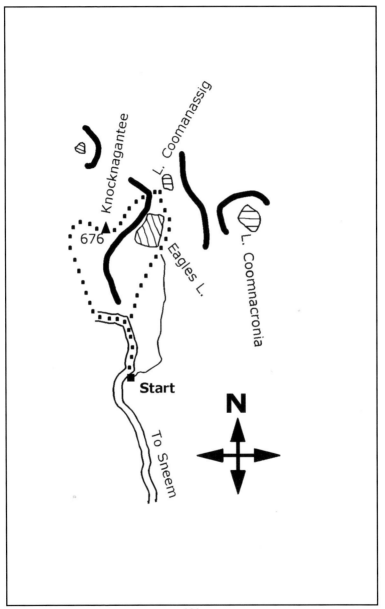

*The short, but impressive, east ridge of Knocknagantee starts
at the small lake of Coomanassig, above the waterfall.*

ROUTE 26
CAHERCONREE/DERRYMORE – THE NORTH-EAST BUTTRESS

Distance: 9km   *Ascent:* 775m
Time: 4.5 hrs.   *Terrain: Easy* to *Hard* scrambling
Ref.: O.S. Map 71   *Start:* Q742108
Equipment: 8mm or 9mm rope, slings and karabiners needed.

From Blennerville, on the north side of the Dingle peninsula, drive 8km west on the N86, and turn left up a narrow road just after Derrymore Bridge. Drive for less than 1km up this road, ascending a little and park where the road turns sharply left.

Go right and follow a road which quickly becomes a path, keeping the houses on the right, and walk for just over 100m as far as a gate. Go through the gate onto open ground, and walk in a south-easterly direction to the entrance to the glen, staying on the west side, keeping the river on the left. Follow a path for 3km into the glen, past the three lakes to the base of the north-east facing buttress which is located in the south-western corner of the coum. There is a distinctive gully on the left, and a green, open couloir on the right.

The easiest approach is to stay on the right, intermittent *Easy* scrambling at first. Navigation is straightforward and the further left, closer to the gully, the more technical the terrain. The buttress is a mix of grass and rock, so it is best to climb this in dry conditions. As height is gained, the ground becomes a little more problematic, and the scrambling more consistent, *Easy* to *Moderate* with occasional *Hard* scramble moves. Reach a crag, and follow it around to the right, walking on slabs and stepping over two deep openings.

Follow the wall up a grass ramp until the height lessens. An *Easy* scramble move in a short gully exits above the crag. Continue on mixed scrambling and numerous choices of more technical rock if preferred. The stratification and erosion of the rock are vertical, which does not provide obvious foot- or hand-

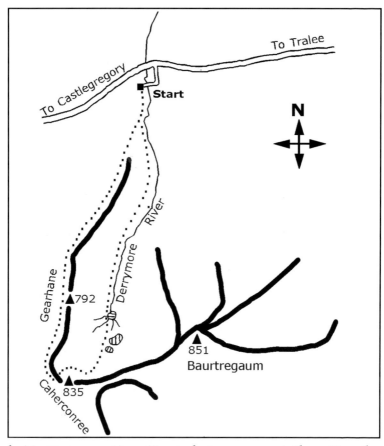

holds. However, side-pulling techniques are useful here. Near the top, another crag can be avoided by moving to the right, and around it, *Easy* to *Moderate* scrambling, and on to less steep, scree-covered ground. Arrive at a point approximately 100m to the right of Caherconree peak.

Walk in a north-northeast direction to Gearhane and then change direction slightly to the northeast and descend beyond the entrance of the glen. Reach the path, and return as originally approached.

The north-east buttress, beneath Caherconree, provides numerous scrambling and climbing options after a long approach up the Derrymore Glen.

ROUTE 27
COUMANARE – NORTH-EAST RIDGE / GULLY

Distance: 4km   *Ascent*: 520m
Time: 4 hrs   *Terrain*: *Easy* to *Hard* scrambling, *V. Diff* to *Severe*
                        rockclimbing
Ref.: O.S. Map 70   *Start:* Q514078
Equipment: 9mm or 11mm rope, rockclimbing equipment, harness, slings, helmet and karabiners needed.

Descend the Connor Pass road northeastwards and park in a lay-by on the right, approximately 4km from the pass, on the north side of the Dingle peninsula. Leave the road and contour around the northeast spur and descend to Lough Camclaun. Walk on the west bank, beyond where the lake narrows perceptibly to a point opposite a small island in the lake. Ascend steep ground to the base of an obvious ridge, with a shallow gully on its right. To avoid the boulder field below the ridge, it is advisable to approach the ridge diagonally from the right.

The ridge can be climbed directly, and the first pitch is short and looks harder than it is, at *Severe* rockclimbing. Climb directly, initially, before moving to the left, to a good belay stance under a nose. The second pitch is easier, at *V. Diff* but poorly protected, and finding a good belay position can be problematic. *Diff* climbing and consistent, mixed scrambling from here on up, but it is poorly protected and very exposed. Dry conditions are essential to do this safely, so if not, then move into the gully, which is just steep ground with occasional *Easy* scrambling. The gully and ridge finish less than halfway up and the ground is very broken.

Continue climbing, following a diagonal line along crags on the right. Encounter mixed, inconsistent scrambling, becoming easier near the top. Exit just south of the summit, at 670m. Descend north for just over a kilometre to meet the road and back to the start. Though the *ascent* and *distance* are short, the route needs a minimum of 4 hrs because the *terrain* is varied and can be problematic.

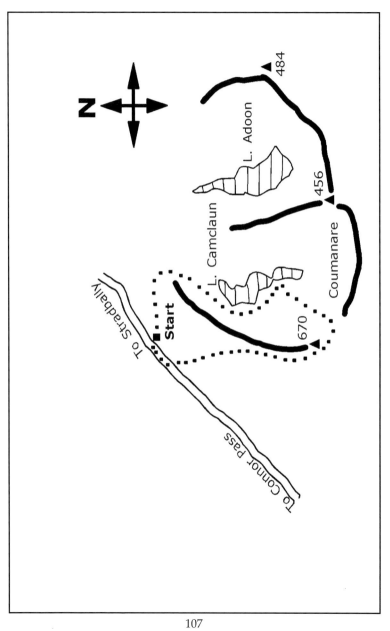

A difficult, but short, rockclimbing ridge above Lough Camclaun Lake can be bypassed by going into the gully to its right.

ROUTE 28
BRANDON PEAK – EAST RIDGE

Distance: 6km   *Ascent:* 780m
Time: 5 hrs   *Terrain: Easy* to *Hard* scrambling.
Ref.: O.S. Map 70   *Start*: Q491085
Equipment: 9mm or 11mm rope, full range of climbing equipment, helmet and harness needed.

Just before the village of Cloghane, on the north side of the Dingle peninsula, turn left and drive for 3km as far as a bridge. Park the car just off the road, turn right and begin walking up a track. Pass a farmhouse on the right and go through a gate. Walk up the track towards Lough Avoonane. Contour around to the right, staying low and west of the Owenmore river which flows out of Lough Cruttia. There is a distinct path on the western side of the lake. Walk for about one-quarter the length of the lake before turning left and ascending a broad gully on the east face of Brandon Peak.

Ascend the gully to avoid the initial section of the ridge. On reaching a massive slab in the gully, move out to the right to begin the scrambling section at an elevation of 400m.

The portion of the ridge to be climbed is between 400m and 550m and though not long, it provides some of the finest scrambling and mountain climbing in the country on surprisingly good rock. A good option to begin the climb is a slab of rock, 15m high with a crack running to the top. It is at *V. Diff* rockclimbing standard and is well protected though placement of pieces can zig-zag a little. This enjoyable start to the ridge offers a sense of exposure in a well-protected environment. The scrambling is consistent and mixed from here on with many harder options to tackle if preferred.

The ridge finishes at an elevation of 550m and from here to the top it is just a pleasant walk to the summit of Brandon Peak at 840m with magnificent views of the coum between Brandon Peak and Dromnamucka.

From the summit move southwest to Gearhane and descend

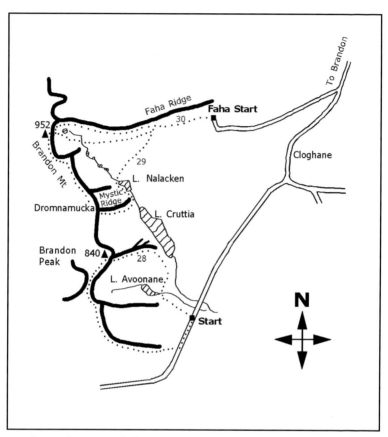

south-southeast and then east on an obvious spur. Avoid steep ground near the bottom by turning northeast and also avoid a forest plantation to emerge on to the road a couple of hundred metres from the start.

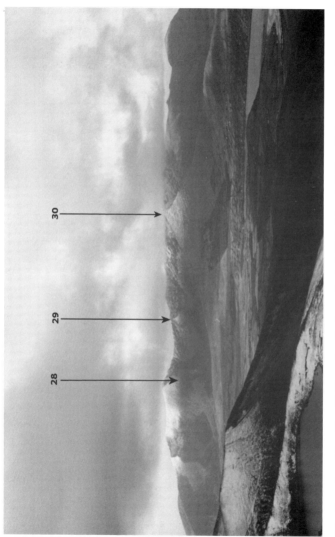

The Brandon Massif, with Brandon Peak on the left (28), Mystic Ridge (29) centre, and Brandon Mountain (30) on the right. This photograph was taken from the summit of Beenoskee.

ROUTE 29
BRANDON MOUNTAIN – MYSTIC RIDGE

Distance: 9km   *Ascent:* 850m
Time: 7 hrs   *Terrain: Easy* to *Hard* scrambling, *Diff, V. Diff*
                          and *Severe* rockclimbing.
Ref.: O.S. Map 70   *Start*: Q493119
Equipment: 9mm or 11mm rope, full range of rockclimbing equipment,
helmet and harness needed.

On the north side of the Dingle peninsula, drive through the village of Cloghane for 1.5km and turn left on a narrow road. There is a signpost for Brandon Mountain at the turn-off. Ascend this road as far as it goes, and park on the right. Walk along a track behind the farmhouse, through a gate and onto open ground. Turn right and walk to the grotto. Follow a well-worn path which is also marked by direction posts. Walk to the highest point on the track before leaving it and descend southwest between the second and third lakes with the waterfall on the right. On reaching the glen, avoid the north-east-facing crag directly in front by descending a little to the left and when level with the start of the second lake, scramble around the crag and ascend to the base of the ridge.

There will be some intermittent *Easy* scrambling on this section. The ridge starts at an elevation of 500m and rises to the highest point between Brandon Peak and Brandon Mountain at 750m. Where the stone wall meets the crag is the easiest and most logical start and a number of options are available with nothing below *V. Diff* for the initial move. This first move on rock becomes a short grass slope leading to a crag and an obvious slab on the right. Belay the Second to this point. The slab is a *Severe* rockclimbing move with excellent protection, solid handholds though nothing much for the feet. Move right on this and then left above the slab. Belay the Second after a short run out as communication and rope management can be difficult otherwise. Move roped up

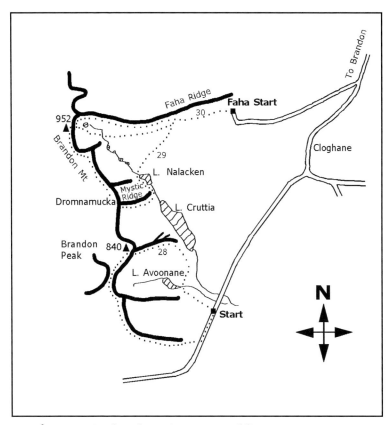

together on mixed and consistent scrambling.

Reach an obvious crag and move to the right, to a gully. Though the gully can be wet and messy looking, it is the easier option to get over this crag. It has good protection on the right and is graded as *Severe* rockclimbing. Halfway up is a good stance for belaying and beyond this the gully is steep grass with a *Hard* scramble move out. To avoid the next crag move down and to the left and scramble around it. The ground becomes a little problematic here. It is steep and the easier option is around the middle (as one faces it) on a mixture of grass and rock, *Moderate* rockclimbing. After this, avoid a crag on the right and ascend a steep,

*Mystic Ridge, as seen descending from
the Faha path into the glen between
Lough Nalacken and Lough Cruttia.*

grassy ramp on the left. This is one of the good reasons not to tackle Mystic Ridge in wet conditions. Above the ramp, move to the right again, with mixed and consistent scrambling to the top, which is not far away.

From the top, walk northwest for the summit of Brandon Mountain, which is over 1km away. Descend northwards a short distance to meet the path from Faha. Descend steep ground into the coum where the paternoster lakes begin. Follow the track and cross the stream. The track follows the line of the Faha Ridge on its lower slopes and ascends a little before descending to the grotto and back to the start.

ROUTE 30
BRANDON MOUNTAIN – THE FAHA RIDGE

Distance: 7.5km   *Ascent:* 800m
Time: 4.5 hrs   *Terrain: Easy* to *Hard* scrambling, and two short
            sections of *V. Diff* rockclimbing.
Ref.: O.S. Map 70   *Start*: Q493119
Equipment: 9mm rope, slings, 2 x extenders, rocks 1 to 7, and karabiners
needed

On the north side of the Dingle peninsula, drive through the village of Cloghane for 1.5km and turn left on a narrow road. There is a signpost for Brandon Mountain at the turn-off. Ascend this road as far as it goes and park on the right. Walk along a track behind the farmhouse, through a gate and onto open ground. Turn right and walk to the grotto. Follow a well-worn path which is also marked by direction posts. Walk to the high point of the track before leaving it and ascending the ridge to the right.

It is gentle and grassy at first, but becomes more exposed and rocky after passing the ruins of the promontory fort at 882m. The views into the Owennafeana River valley on the right, and the paternoster lakes on the left between the Brandon Peak / Brandon Mountain ridge and the Faha ridge, are spectacular. Sections of *Easy* to *Moderate* scrambling will eventually lead to a short, knife-edge section. There is a vertical drop to a col from this, so to avoid having to abseil off, climb down to the col on the right before the knife-edge section. From the col continue to climb the ridge to a short pinnacle of about 5m high which is *V. Diff* rock and can be adequately protected. There is just one further short, low move of *V. Diff* which can also be protected and after this it is just *Easy* to *Moderate* scrambling to the top at 891m.

If a direct climb on the ridge is to be avoided then an alternative is to go around the ridge by back-climbing down from the col to the north (*Moderate* scramble move) and ascend on steep ground with the ridge on the left. There will be some intermittent

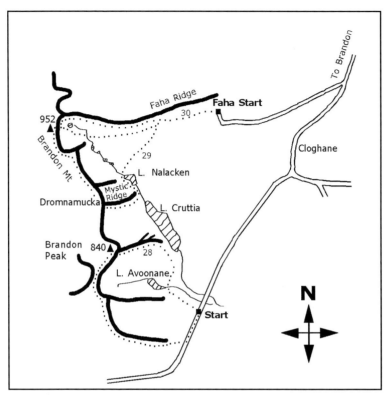

Easy scrambling on the way up. From the top, walk south to the summit of Brandon Mountain 500m away. On the way to the summit, the path from Faha meets this ridge. The summit is marked by the ruins of St Brendan's Oratory. Because Brandon Mountain is so close to the sea, the full height is appreciated and the panorama of sea and landscape worth the effort. From the summit, walk northwards, back to the path and descend steep ground, following the path into the coum where the paternoster lakes begin. Follow the track and cross the stream following the line of the Faha Ridge on its lower slopes. Ascend a little to the highest point of the track, descend to the grotto and back to the start.

The Faha Ridge, taken from Lough Cruttia, makes a varied and fine approach to Brandon Mountain.

MORE FROM THIS PRESS

The Way I went:
An Irishman in Ireland
Robert Lloyd Praeger
New Introduction by Michael Viney

Written by Ireland's greatest field botanist and first published in 1937, Robert Praeger's personal tour of Ireland's natural wonders has had a greater influence on Irish naturalists than any other book. It represents five years of weekends spent walking the countryside, swimming through flooded caverns, staying all night on islands, sifting fossil bones, and exploring cattle-tramped tombs.

1-898256-35-7 PB £11.99 1997 b/w photographs

Companion Guide to Ireland
Brendan Lehane

In this revised and updated edition, an acknowledged expert concentrates on history, culture, architecture and art. This information-packed guide reads like the best of travel writing, always interesting and charming, sometimes eccentric.

1-903464-08-0 PB £15.00 colour b/w photos and maps

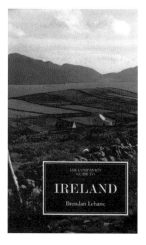

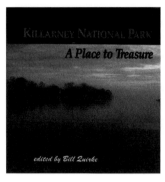

Killarney National Park:
A Place to Treasure
Edited by Bill Quirke

Killarney National Park, with its lakes, woods and mountains, forms the backdrop for most visits to Kerry. Despite the popular image of a commercialised tourist destination, the National Park is probably the greatest natural treasury in Ireland, remaining relatively undiscovered and unspoiled. Each contributor to this book is an expert on the different aspects of the Park.

1-898256-69-1 HB £25.00 colour and b/w photos

New Irish Walks and Scrambles
The Burren, Aran Islands and County Clare
Barry Keane

The walks described vary from pleasant strolls to more strenuous walks. Most of these have not featured in previous guidebooks and so provide a range of new options.

1-898256-83-7 PB £5.99 b/w maps

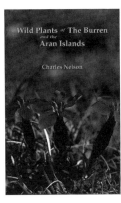

Wild Plants of the Burren and Aran Islands
Charles E. Nelson

The Burren and Aran Islands are renowned for the beauty of their natural flora. Charles Nelson has selected 120 of the most widely occurring plus a number of special plants. Introduced with background information on the plants and instructions on how to use the guide, photographs are grouped according to flower colour and the pages colour coded. Plants are described simply using the common English name, followed by the name in Irish and then the Latin (botanical) name. The flowering period and each plant's distribution are given.

1-898256-70-5 PB £10.00 full colour

Flora Hibernica
A Guide to the Wild Flowers, Plants and Trees of Ireland
Jonathan Pilcher and Valerie Hall

Combining the latest information from modern and ancient Irish botanical studies, the book describes the very special landscape and plant combinations of this damp and diverse land. Beginning with an introductory overview of the past and present, it then describes, chapter by chapter, the plants associated with specific habitats such as the seashore, woodlands, boglands, etc. Each chapter is profusely illustrated in colour.

1-903464-05-6 HB £25 full colour (October 2001)

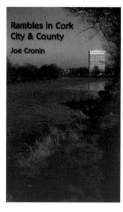

Rambles in Cork City and County
Joe Cronin

Cork is blessed with fine walking potential. This book features over 30 rambles in town and country. Most are from 3-5 miles, all are accessible to young and old, fit and unfit. Features include flora and fauna, history, archaeology and folklore, from the Gearagh's unique ecosystem to the thirteenth-century Church of St Multose in Kinsale.

1-898256-72-1 PB £7.99

Cape Clear, Island Magic
A Photographic, Historical and Dramatic Account of Clear Island
Chuck Kruger

Upstate New York resident Chuck Kruger bought a farm on Clear Island, County Cork, in 1986 and moved his family there. This is his personal portrait of the island: 'Cape's a poem I read every day, every night. It's a point of reference, a metaphor by which I confrim my very being. It's the place I love more than any other.'

1-898256-01-2 PB £7.99 b/w photographs